INTRODUCTION TO THE
TECHNIQUE OF PSYCHOTHERAPY

D1716330

ABOUT THE AUTHOR

Dr. Samuel I. Greenberg is a psychiatrist and psychoanalyst who teaches at the University of Florida and is a consultant at the Veterans Affairs Medical Center in Gainesville, Florida.

Soon after he received and M.D. from the University of Chicago (Rush), he was called up for service with the Army Medical Corps in World War II. Returning after five years, he began psychiatric training at New York University Bellevue Medical Center and later, psychoanalytic training at the Karen Horney Psychoanalytic Center in New York City.

After years of private practice in New York and Miami, he was appointed Visiting Professor at the University of Florida and Chief, Mental Health Clinic at the affiliated V.A. Medical Center. He has contributed to professional journals as well as to popular publications. He is the author of *Neurosis Is a Painful Style of Living* (New American Library) and *Euthanasia and Assisted Suicide: Psychosocial Issues* (Charles C Thomas).

He and Rose, his wife for over forty years, live in Gainesville, Florida, with their three cats.

INTRODUCTION TO THE TECHNIQUE OF PSYCHOTHERAPY

Practice Guidelines for Psychotherapists

By

SAMUEL I. GREENBERG, M.D., F.A.P.A.

Clinical Professor in Psychiatry, University of Florida
Consultant, V.A. Medical Center
Gainesville, Florida

Foreword by

Ronald Alan Shellow, M.D., F.A.C.P., F.A.P.A.

CHARLES C THOMAS · PUBLISHER, LTD.
Springfield · Illinois · U.S.A.

Published and Distributed Throughout the World by

CHARLES C THOMAS • PUBLISHER, LTD.
2600 South First Street
Springfield, Illinois 62794-9265

© *1998 by* CHARLES C THOMAS • PUBLISHER, LTD.
ISBN 0-398-06904-2 (paper)
ISBN 0-398-06905-0 (cloth)

Library of Congress Catalog Card Number: 98-27916

With THOMAS BOOKS *careful attention is given to all details of manufacturing
and design. It is the Publisher's desire to present books that are satisfactory as to their
physical qualities and artistic possibilities and appropriate for their particular use.*
THOMAS BOOKS *will be true to those laws of quality that assure a good name
and good will.*

Printed in the United States of America
CR-R-3

Library of Congress Cataloging in Publication Data
Greenberg, Samuel I., 1912-
    Introduction to the technique of psychotherapy : practice
guidelines for psychotherapists / by Samuel I. Greenberg ;
foreword by Ronald Alan Shellow.
        p.   cm.
    Includes bibliographical references and index.
    ISBN 0-398-06904-2 (cloth). -- ISBN 0-398-06905-0 (paper)
    1. Psychodynamic psychotherapy. 2. Psychotherapy--Practice.
I. Title.
    [DNLM: 1. Psychotherapy--methods. 2. Practice Guidelines. WM
420 G7985i 1998]
RC 489.P72G74   1998
616.89'14--dc21
DNLM/DLC
for Library of Congress   98-27916
                                                                              CIP

For Rose

FOREWORD

I met Sam soon after he moved to Miami. It did not take long before the community recognized his talents as a clinician and as a dynamic teacher interested in education for all the mental health disciplines. In a relatively short space of time, he was elected President of the South Florida Psychiatric Society and Founding President of the Behavioral Science Institute.

Mainly, it was as a practitioner, teacher, and supervisor of psychotherapy that I developed the greatest respect for Sam Greenberg. He practiced his own brand of analytic/dynamic psychotherapy. It was based, not slavishly, on the teachings of Karen Horney, but it was mostly Sam Greenberg. His psychotherapy was comprehensive, eclectic, optimistic, practical, and effective. The same year I met Sam, Bernard Glueck—who had been an expert alienist for Clarence Darrow in his defense of Leopold and Loeb—said, "I no longer advise patients to wait until after their analysis to marry. When I first began psychoanalysis, analysis took a few months, and marriages lasted forever. But, now it is the other way around." Sam's treatment was long-term by today's standards, but it did not last forever. His patients got better, and many of them maintained their improvements, after only a few months of psychotherapy.

As teacher and supervisor, Sam listened very carefully to what his students said and did, just as with his patients. Although he indicates in the book that he is not an admirer of DSM-IV (He and I differ on this), he is, in reality, a good psychiatric diagnostician. He tells us how he does it—by having a format in mind, taking a comprehensive history, and a careful, observing examination of the patient. He then advises on how to conduct psychotherapy with various patients and with special consideration of certain problems.

As always, he is free to tell us what he did, by example, to his pupils what to do and what not to do. If a reader speaks with many psychotherapists, he will find most are secretive about what they really do in the privacy of their offices. Sam is not. He tells us what he does clearly and concisely. He tells us how he conducts psychotherapy. He says it directly, no fuss, no fanfare. Just like Sam Greenberg.

The book is clear enough to instruct, without frightening, a beginning therapist. It is complicated enough to allow the experienced psychotherapist to gain a few "pearls." Some years ago, in an informal consultation, I told Sam of an intervention I had made with a patient. He responded by saying, "If you don't know what to say, you are better off keeping your mouth shut." It was good supervision, and I never forgot it. It is in the book, a little gentler, but it is there.

And, I believe it will help another generation of psychotherapists who practice in an environment of managed care which discourages this type of therapy. I predict that if one follows Samuel Greenberg's psychotherapy, responds to case managers with words similar to those he gives us, and allows results with patients to demonstrate the efficacy, the therapist will get approvals and get paid for helping patients in this way.

RONALD A. SHELLOW, M.D., F.A.C.P.,, F.A.P.A.
Formerly, Speaker, American Psychiatric Association
Assembly of District Branches
Clinical Professor in Psychiatry, University of Miami

PREFACE

There are now many fine books on psychotherapy, but the author felt that a basic, simply written book, with a minimum of theory, would be helpful to the beginning therapist. This is a practical book and I tell what I do. I have tried to capture the informal tone of an older therapist talking to one who is just starting out. It is a short book, not comprehensive, that includes only the more important issues that I have learned in 40 years of study, practice, and teaching. I learned most from my mistakes, and those of my colleagues.

The emphasis is on individual, dynamic psychotherapy. Once these fundamentals are learned, then technical procedures from the other theoretical approaches that have proven helpful can be added to the therapist's repertoire. There are no pure forms of psychotherapy. In time, each therapist will develop her own style depending on her temperament and training. Some techniques she will follow exactly, modify some and reject others. No therapist can do everything well, nor be comfortable with all patients.

Psychodynamic therapy is the legacy of the psychoanalytic movement. It is known by a variety of names: analytically-oriented, uncovering, expressive, interpersonal, etc. Psychoanalysis made monumental contributions to the understanding of human character and motivation, and to therapy. Unfortunately, the classical technique was rigidly applied and slavishly followed the original experimental model. Even so, it helped many.

Freud has been criticized for the last 100 years, but we are all in his debt for the great contributions: that feelings and behavior may be determined by unconscious forces (what you don't know can hurt you), the crucial importance of childhood, the special importance of sexual development for neurosis, and that dreams are meaningful.

Dynamic psychotherapy is based on these fundamental concepts, but the technique has been modified to conform to the scientific and economic temper of the times. We have learned to use time, and money, more carefully. A last comment: I use the old-fashioned term *neurosis* instead of the politically correct mental disorder. The DSM's are useful for research and insurance reports, but in therapy we treat a whole person, not one divided into Axes I-V.

S.I.G.

ACKNOWLEDGMENTS

I have been studying all my life and am indebted to many teachers. My patients not only paid me, they also taught me. Most of all, I feel indebted to the teachers and colleagues at the American Institute For Psychoanalysis in New York which was founded by Karen Horney.

I am grateful to many friends and colleagues who have given generously of their time and provided valuable feed back. Especially do I wish to thank Susan Walen, Linda Provus McElroy, Robert Hornberger, Frank Sieka, Ross McElroy, John Kuldau, and Ben Greenberg.

Thanks also to Michael P. Thomas, Virginia Meyers, William H. Bried, and the editors at Charles C Thomas, Ltd. Their help is much appreciated.

Acknowledgement is gratefully made to the *American Journal of Psychoanalysis* for permission to quote from my paper, "Analysis once A Week," 46:327-335, 1986.

CONTENTS

IRREVERENT OBSERVATIONS

The unconscious contains the theories of the analyst.

Meyer Maskin
Late, Professor of Psychiatry,
Emeritus, University of Florida

You always know who the patient is—
he's the one who pays the other fellow.

Harold Kelman
Late, Dean, American Institute for
Psychoanalysis, Karen Horney
Center, New York

INTRODUCTION TO THE
TECHNIQUE OF PSYCHOTHERAPY

PART 1
BASIC PSYCHOTHERAPY

Chapter 1

INTRODUCTION

Beginning therapists sometimes ask older ones: "What does a therapist really do?" The answer is: "You listen." This doesn't seem to be a very satisfactory answer; it's so commonplace. Upon reflection, it makes a lot of sense. Therapists are masters of the commonplace, they are professional listeners. This quality of listening is not to be underestimated, it is hard work. It is also rare. Few people really listen to others. We live in a world full of noise, people talking and shouting at each other, but not really listening. Also, in therapy, a unique relationship is developing between the talker and the listener.

The psychotherapist gives the patient her full attention in a setting that tries for a minimum of distraction. She usually doesn't even answer the phone during the session. The therapist wants to learn: what kind of person is this man who wants help?—what is he out for? —what's wrong with him?—what's right with him? She listens not only to the words, but to the person. The therapist tries to put aside her own prejudices and listen with an open mind, no axe to grind. Is the patient frightened, angry, depressed, frustrated, arrogant or burdened by self-contempt? An important result of the process is that the patient begins to listen to himself.

Of course, the therapist does much more than listen. He observes how the patient talks, dresses, moves, and so on. He encourages the patient to speak freely, and he asks questions. He wants to know the story of the patient's life. Above all, the therapist wants to develop a helping, nonjudgmental relationship where the patient feels free to talk about things he never faced before. He is not alone, he has a therapist who also is interested in understanding the things that worry him.

Therapists also help the patient develop insight by their interpretations and, when appropriate, give support, reassurance and advice. We have learned much about human character and motivation in the last hundred years. While each patient is unique, we can safely assume that he or she shares many traits in common with all other human beings. We don't have to approach each new patient as a research project that has never been done before.

It is wise to proceed cautiously. We don't like to make mistakes at any time, but especially at the beginning, mistakes are costly. Respect the tenacity of chronic symptoms; the patient has not been able to solve them in all this time. Until you know a great deal about the patient, don't rush in with answers to problems which have plagued him for many years. It is safe to assume that behind every question may be a problem. You can say: "We'll try to find out." You can also answer, with a question.

The therapist is not obligated to cure the patient. Depressions, phobias, panic attacks, unhappy marriages, destructive life-styles and all the other symptoms for which patients seek help are usually not resolved quickly. That happens regularly in books and the movies, but rarely in real life. Sometimes, they will not be resolved at all. The therapist is responsible only to see that the patient receives careful, competent treatment. The beginning therapist would like to achieve quick results; it would be reassuring for him. It usually doesn't happen.

DEFINITIONS

A simple definition of psychotherapy is that it is treatment by psychological means. A more formal definition is that of Hans Strupp: "Psychotherapy is an interpersonal process designed to bring about modification of feelings, cognition, attitudes and/or behavior which have proved troublesome to the person seeking help from a trained professional."

Psychotherapy may be with individuals, couples, families or groups. The theoretical approaches vary and carry many designations: supportive, uncovering, expressive, analytically-oriented, interpersonal, cognitive, behavioral "Rational-Emotive," Gestalt, and so on.

In actual practice, there are no pure forms. The therapist adapts the treatment to the patient, what she needs and what she can use. Competent therapists of all the different schools help patients. The therapist keeps her theories to herself; they help her organize the data for evaluation and treatment, but she doesn't burden the patient with them. Almost all forms of psychotherapy have several elements in common: a supportive and helping relationship, an opportunity for self-expression, and a more constructive way of thinking about problems.

VARIETIES OF THERAPY

There have been a confusing profusion of therapies. This country has had not only junk foods, but also junk therapies. Suffering patients hope for quick relief and have followed many charismatic individuals who have promised better and quicker results. Over the years, we have had encounter groups, marathons, Dianetics, primal scream therapy, "est," Gestalt therapy and transactional analysis, among others. Some of the approaches had merit, many did not, and after a period of popularity, they faded away. Hypnosis and hypnotherapy have limited value in my opinion. The role of the patient is too passive, he is not an active partner in working out solutions to his problems. There are very few therapists who use hypnosis effectively; again this is my opinion.

There are three major approaches of merit: the psychodynamic (also called analytic, expressive and interpersonal), the cognitive and the behavioral. The last two are often combined. There are no pure forms of therapy; in actual practice elements of all are combined. In Behavior Therapy, the focus is on observable behavior, and the aim is to modify current symptoms that interfere with the individual's adaptive functioning. It is based on learning theory and designs individual treatment programs tailored to specific problems. It has been useful in the treatment of phobias and compulsions.

Cognitive Therapy focuses on the conscious reactions of the individual to the upsetting problems. The patient (client) is asked to report on her beliefs, assumptions and expectations about herself, the world and the future. These have been called the "cognitive triad." Therapy proceeds more quickly because the emphasis is on conscious (and preconscious) mental events and current happenings. It does not emphasize dreams nor attempt to bring unconscious material into awareness. Many therapists make effective use of this approach. Analytically-trained therapists would consider it the domain of ego psychology.

Above all, therapy involves a working alliance between two human beings and the help that one human being can give to another. It is most desirable that the therapist not intrude her personal traits and prejudices into the relationship, but it also is not possible for her to be completely anonymous or a "blank screen." Common sense will not resolve neurotic problems, but there is a place for it in the relationship between patient and therapist.

RECOMMENDED READING

1. Basch, M.F.: *Practicing Psychotherapy—A Casebook.* Basic Books, 1992.
2. Dewald, P.A.: *Psychotherapy—A Dynamic Approach.* Second Edition. Basic Books, 1971.
3. Dobson, K.S. (Ed): *Handbook of Cognitive—Behavioral Therapies.* New York, Guilford Press, 1988.
4. Frank, J.D., & Frank, J.B.: *Persuasion and Healing.* 3rd Edition, Baltimore, Johns Hopkins University Press, 1991.
5. Gabbard, G.O.: *Psychodynamic Psychiatry In Clinical Practice.* DSM IV Edition. Washington, American Psychiatric Press, 1994.
6. Greenson, R.R.: *The Technique and Practice of Psychoanalysis.* Vol. 1, New York, International Universities Press, 1967.
7. Wallerstein, R.S.: *The Talking Cures—The Psychoanalyses and the Psychotherapies.* New Haven, Yale University Press, 1996.
8. Yalom, I.D.: *Existential Psychotherapy.* New York, Basic Books, 1980.

Chapter 2

THE INITIAL INTERVIEW

The initial interview is a meeting between two strangers, and stressful for both. This is a busy time for the therapist, he has much to do, but most important of all is the relationship he wants with the new patient. He wants to come across as a helpful and competent professional who knows what he is doing.

In all encounters between people, a good first impression is very desirable. It is especially important in therapy. A good beginning goes a long way toward establishing a productive therapeutic alliance. A poor beginning may doom the therapy; even if it doesn't, it makes the going much more difficult.

In the eagerness of the therapist to get all the information he needs, he may pressure the patient and increase his anxiety. This is a common mistake. The needs of the therapist to evaluate and diagnose should not have higher priority than the needs of the patient. It is often due to the insecurity or rigidity of the therapist. A safe assumption to make is that the patient needs more help than the therapist. The patient is the one struggling with the problems; the therapist can be more objective about them.

The initial interview offers a great opportunity to observe: how the patient looks, dresses, moves, talks, and so on. First impressions are important. Nurture them, they can tell you a great deal about this person. What is your predominant response to this patient: compassion, wanting to help, liking or disliking, irritation, fear, uneasiness? Sometimes it is helpful to "forget" that this is a patient; how would you feel about this person if you met him/her at a social gathering? What you feel about the patient is also how many others feel about him.

Patients are eager for help with their problems and most have a lot to say at the first meeting. If they start speaking spontaneously, keep quiet, and listen. Quiet, attentive listening provides a great deal of implicit support. The therapist only needs to nod occasionally or make some brief comment to keep the narrative going. Other patients may not know where to start and need guidance. The current situation is usually a good place to start and then continue with questions which should not be too upsetting. Usually it is easier for the patient to talk about interpersonal issues, about significant others: spouse, friends, employer, colleagues, etc. It is harder to talk about himself.

A few patients may pour out such a tale of horror that you begin to feel overwhelmed. Sometimes there can be too much abreaction. They provide too much information, too quickly, accompanied by intense emotion. It is then wise to slow the process, give the patient a Kleenex and steer the conversation into more neutral topics. If the current situation is too disturbing, then go back to the past. The therapist can switch topics by saying something like: "What you are saying is important and we'll get back to it, but right now I would like to know about this other matter." The therapist "conducts" the interview. Like a conductor of an orchestra, the therapist can alter the tempo and rhythm depending on the patient's emotional state.

OBJECTIVES OF THE INITIAL INTERVIEW

No two initial interviews are exactly alike and there is no "standard" manner of conducting them, but the therapist knows the data he would like to obtain and so has an overall plan in mind. At a minimum, he wants to get a clear picture of the presenting complaints and an outline of the life history. The therapist is also trying to evaluate (diagnose) the extent of the pathology as well as the resources of the patient. He would like to get an idea as to how to start. Does the patient need support or is he ready for some interpretation of the presenting complaint. It is often helpful simply to restate the problem in other terms.

Don't assume that the patient's words mean the same thing to him that they do to you. Much later in the course of therapy you may understand what some words mean to the patient. And only then will you get a clear picture and understand what the patient meant. As Humpty Dumpty says in *Alice's Adventures In Wonderland*: "words mean what I want them to mean." To a greater or lesser extent, all individuals operate in a similar manner.

Some patients are impatient with questions. They want answers and resent all those questions. Or they may feel that the questions are "putting them on the spot" and that they have to defend themselves. This is especially true for patients burdened with guilt. Other patients are naive and believe that psychiatrists can "read them like a book" and immediately know what their problems are. When patients are in great need, they tend to see their doctors as "magic helpers" endowed with extraordinary talents and abilities. It may be helpful for the therapist to simply point out that he asks questions to get information.

The therapist tries to understand the reasons for seeking help and what he or she expects from treatment. What does he want or need? Was it his idea to come or was he pushed or coerced ("Unless you get straightened out, I'm leaving!")? Does he think this is a waste of time? Does he expect that two or three sessions will provide answers to all the problems or has he heard that this can go on for years? Inquire about previous therapy; it often provides valuable information. If it was successful, what was most helpful? If unsuccessful, what did the patient object to? ("He just sat and listened and didn't do a thing!") There is a great advantage to being the second (or third) therapist, you benefit from the previous experience. We learn a lot from mistakes.

To summarize the objectives of the initial interview, we try to obtain:

1. a fairly clear picture of the presenting complaints,
2. an outline of the life history,
3. reasons for seeking treatment, and
4. expectations from treatment,
5. evaluation of the extent of the pathology and of the resources available to the patient.

DECISIONS

The therapist has many important decisions to make at this time. Do you want him for a patient or should you refer him? You don't need to like every patient, but you should be clear as to how you feel about him. If there are strong feelings of dislike which you cannot account for, it may be wise to consider referring the patient. If there is a very strong physical attraction, it may also be wise to refer her or him to a colleague.

All options should be considered. Is this patient a good candidate for dynamic psychotherapy? Does he need medication or hospitalization? Would he do better in group therapy or couple/marital therapy? Should he be referred to AA or some other special facility?

If the decision is made to keep the patient, then the therapist needs to decide how to start. Does he need support at this time? Is he in such trouble that he needs help just keeping his head above water? Or can you start analyzing (clarifying) some problem. If the patient is ready for it, great relief of anxiety follows from analyzing a problem so that he or she has a better understanding of what is going on. What is the danger? Why is the patient unable to deal with it?

It is usually wise not to reassure too quickly if the patient can tolerate the anxiety. You don't really know the patient and all the facts. Patients may experience some relief since he is no longer struggling alone; he now has a therapist who can help him. At times, the level of anxiety is so great that reassurance is indicated. Although the patient feels better, the problem has been covered up. Sometime further along in the course of therapy it will require more work to uncover it again so that it may be dealt with.

It will take experience and judgement to decide how much anxiety is optimum. A certain level of anxiety moves treatment along, the patient wants to get better. However, severe anxiety usually blocks treatment and only support is possible until the level of anxiety is reduced.

It is most desirable that the therapist not make mistakes, especially in this first meeting. Mistakes of omission are less conspicuous than those of commission. A good rule of thumb for the therapist about to make some comment: "If in doubt, don't."

With all this to do, how can a therapist accomplish it in one session? Usually he can't. Many times the work of the initial interview requires several meetings. However, it is well for the therapist to keep in mind the outline of what he is trying to accomplish. This may communicate itself to the patient that there is a method to all this, it is not just casual conversation.

PRACTICAL CONSIDERATIONS

It is a good idea to stop five or ten minutes before the time is up to allow the patient to ask questions. In his eagerness to get all the data, the therapist may use up all the time. "We'll continue next week" may not be a very satisfactory way to end the first session. The patient has waited a long time before coming into therapy and may have questions he would like answered. A week is a long time to wait when you're in pain.

The patient may want to know: Can you help me? "Am I losing my mind?" "What does treatment involve?" Leave enough time in the initial interview to deal with these important concerns. It may be very reassuring to the patient to know that he can be seen as an office patient, or that he does not need medication. A tentative outline of how you want to proceed is also reassuring. For most, this is a first encounter with a "shrink," and they do not know what to expect.

Patients may ask questions which you cannot answer. Do not make extravagant promises and never lie. You are not obligated to tell him more of the truth than he can handle, but do not lie. Unfortunately, we live in a society where liberties are taken with the truth on a vast scale; people do not expect the truth from salesmen, auto mechanics, politicians, and many others. They tend to be more trusting of health professionals, and, in time, most patients will come to trust you.

Note-Taking

Another practical point is about note-taking. Most therapists take extensive notes during the initial interview. The notes of the initial interview are valuable; you will refer to them many times. An anxious patient seeking help will often give you the most valuable information during this first hour. The entire pattern of his neurosis may be captured in these notes. On subsequent visits, the anxiety may be less, the defenses will be up and the patient will be far less open.

It is helpful to refer to the notes at intervals as treatment progresses and especially to compare his current reactions to certain people and events, and how he described them on the first interview. Also, for forensic considerations, *never alter the notes*, they can be a monumental embarrassment should litigation ever be involved. If desirable, make additional notes to clarify some issue, but never change the notes.

Another important consideration is: how does the patient feel about the note-taking? There will be varied reactions. Many will be so preoccupied with their own problems that they will hardly notice. Others may be impressed that you are taking them seriously and writing down what they have to say. Others may feel that you are not really listening to them, you are just taking routine notes as you do in all your cases. Still others may worry about confidentiality; who has access to the notes?

If the patient keeps looking uneasily at the writing pad, his feelings about notes need to be explored. Some patients will speak more freely if you do not take notes. They like the idea that you are looking straight at them and giving them your undivided attention. In these instances, the notes can be written after the session ends. Similar considerations involve tape-recording. I feel it should be avoided, especially the initial sessions. Later sessions may be recorded for teaching purposes after getting the patient's approval, but it unnecessarily complicates the initial interview.

Arrangements, Fees, Return Visits, etc.

In private practice and in some clinics, the therapist will arrange for return visits and fees; in other settings this may be done by a member of the staff. It should be made clear to the patient that sessions are 45 or 50 minutes in length and reserved for the patient. If she cancels without sufficient notice, the time is wasted. In private practice, the patient is usually charged for missed sessions, unless 24 or 48 hours notice is given. This may not be applicable in some managed care organizations or where there is insurance coverage. It is desirable, whenever possible, that return visits be scheduled for the same time each week; it promotes regularity of attendance and avoids confusion.

Try to schedule visits for at least once a week. It is hard to maintain continuity with longer intervals. In the beginning, if possible, twice a week is much better. Also, I address adult patients as: Mr., Mrs., or Ms. This helps establish a professional tone, this is not a casual conversation between two neighbors.

Setting the fee is an area where the neurotic traits of the therapist complicates matters. Some therapists, especially those starting out, have difficulty setting fees. Unsure of their competence, they tend to set fees which are too low. Other therapists, for various reasons, will charge too much. Even where the therapist does not set the fee, he should explore how the patient feels about them. Are they a burden? What does the patient do without in order to pay for treatment? Is the patient reluctant to ask that they be lowered? Some affluent patients who can well afford them, may still resent paying. Money, like sex, is an important topic and the patient's attitudes toward it need to be explored.

How the office is furnished is another important area to be considered. Therapists spend much time in them, and it is desirable that they feel comfortable there. It is also desirable that the patients feel comfortable there. Furnishings which reflect the personality of the therapist in a blatant or intrusive manner may be disturbing.

In the beginning, many patients are so anxious that they pay little attention to the office. However, in time they do note, and react, to how the office is furnished. If the office is very elegant, some may be impressed but others may resent that their fees are paying for this opulence. Patients will also note how the therapist is dressed and make certain inferences from this. The furnishings of the office are very familiar to the therapist, but the patient is seeing them for the first time. The therapist needs to give some thought to how he, and the office, come across to the patient.

If there is a good chance that you may not want the referred person for a patient, it would be kind to let him down gently. Rejections are hard to take. The initial interview can be referred to as a consultation and nothing said explicitly that he would become a regular patient. The reasons given for referral to another therapist may be that he would do better in marital or group therapy, with a behavioral therapist, or that he needs more time than your schedule permits.

SUMMARY

The initial interview is usually very stressful to the patient for whom this is all new. It is also stressful for the therapist who has much to do, and not enough time to do it. The therapist wants to know why the patient is coming, what does he expect from treatment, a clear picture of his presenting problem and something of his background and resources. Does he want him for a patient and where does he start? Also, he tries not to say, or do, anything that will make the patient more uncomfortable than he already is. It is wise not to schedule many new patients on the same day. Also, the work of the initial interview does not have to be completed in one session. Don't rush.

If after the intial consultation (few sessions) you decide not to take this pt - what do you do - he/she might say "You took all this time + now I have to go to someone else + talk about this over again - + answer their questions - can you give them a report?

Chapter 3

LIFE HISTORY

In the initial interview, a brief outline of the patient's life history is usually obtained. However, it is desirable to get as complete a history as circumstances will permit early in the course of therapy. Without this background, the clinical picture of the patient lacks depth. It also is valuable because it gets the patients to thinking about themselves, especially about periods in their lives which they have not thought about in some time. Reviewing the totality of their lives may give a different perspective and better understanding about how they got to be where they are now.

What do you want to get in a life history: facts, an accurate sequence of events, the patient's reactions to those events at the time they occurred, and as she now recalls them. Of course, it is impossible for a patient to experience a past event as she originally experienced it. She is a different person now.

As you are taking the history, you should be alert to the context: Did this come up spontaneously or as elaborations of an answer to your direct questioning? Questions should be worded so that the patient can elaborate on them:

"Tell me about your family?"

"What happened after your parents divorced?"

"What was it like when you came back from Viet Nam?"

We try to avoid questions that can be answered with a simple "yes" or "no." Most patients are looking for help and will be cooperative. They will speak freely if they feel this is what you want them to do, but they often are not sure what is important. They will need questions to guide them. This "guided inquiry" has not been emphasized enough.

Many are not accustomed to expressing themselves and find it hard to do. Nobody ever listened to them at home. With a few patients, nothing is spontaneous; getting a history is like "pulling teeth." The questions need to be frequent and detailed. It may take some patients a long time before they begin to speak with any degree of spontaneity.

AN OUTLINE

Most psychiatric textbooks have a format for the life-history that is appropriate. However, each therapist will modify it so that he is more comfortable with it and finds it more appropriate for his practice. The outline here presented is one which I find helpful for arranging the information I get from patients:

Family History
Childhood and Adolescence
Medical History
Education
Sex and Marriage
Occupation / Career / Military Service
Hobbies / Recreation / Habits / Addictions
Forensic / Antisocial Behavior
Psychiatric History / Suicide Attempts

The above are guidelines, not to be followed slavishly. If the patient is upset by some of the questions, this is noted and the discussion switched to another topic. It can be brought up at another time. As a general rule, patients find it easier to talk about others rather than themselves: spouse, friends, relatives, colleagues, employer, and so on. Although they are talking about others, they are also revealing much about themselves: their likes, dislikes, attitudes, values, ambitions, etc.

Although you need information, never lose sight of the major goal, which is building a good relationship. This is not a police interrogation, don't be heavy-handed. More patients are helped by a good relationship than by brilliant interpretations. Try to cultivate an atmosphere of nonjudgmental acceptance. You ask questions to get information, you only know what the patient tells you.

Family

The family history deserves a lot of attention, its importance cannot be overemphasized. To the young child, her family is the whole world;

she thinks all families are like the one she grew up in and all adults are like her parents.

We try to get a picture of the emotional climate in the family into which this newborn was thrust: warm, stable, loving, or turbulent and hostile. Especially, we try to get a good picture of the relationship between the mother and father. The birth order is important—whether the firstborn, the "baby" in the family, or some place in between. The first born may have responsibilities thrust on her before she is ready. The youngest in the family sometimes remains the "baby" until well into old age.

Many families and cultures value boys differently from girls. In some cultures, a firstborn male is especially privileged. In Italy, pregnant women were often greeted with: "May all your children be males." These attitudes still persist.

Childhood and Adolescence

There is no need to belabor the importance of these crucial periods in the development of the individual. Unfortunate children who suffer repeated illnesses or painful surgical procedures early in life may never fully recover from their effects. Others may compensate for these early frailties and go on to develop into vigorous and dynamic adults (e.g. President Theodore Roosevelt). Also devastating are death, or desertion of a parent, physical and sexual abuse, and neglect.

Adolescence is regularly a difficult transition for many. There are rapid physical, emotional and social changes which are especially difficult in a youth-oriented culture such as ours. The struggles for an identity; independence and social acceptance may be complicated by overindulgence as one extreme and harsh discipline as another. Peers become more important than family. Adolescents may struggle with parents whose values and standards are not appropriate to the contemporary scene. Parents are shocked at the changes which have occurred in their "darling children." Most parents struggle to find a happy mean between overpermissiveness and strict discipline. They can appreciate Freud's comment that: "being a parent is an impossible profession."

Education

Next to the family, school is the most important institution in the formative years of the individual's development. We therefore want to know, not only about the formal academic achievements, but about all other experiences in school. How did he relate to classmates, teachers, extra-curricular events, athletics, etc.? Was there too much pressure to achieve? Is there a history of learning disabilities? These may be troublesome and take years before their ill effects are overcome. Poor schooling in the early grades may leave pupils functionally illiterate and handicapped for the rest of their lives. The best teachers are not the brainiest, but those with human qualities that encourage and stimulate pupils to learn. Unfortunately, we don't value them enough to get and keep the best. Especially in nursery school and the early grades, a good teacher is worth her weight in gold.

Of course, neurotic traits interfere with learning. The excessively anxious student is afraid to ask questions for fear of appearing stupid. He operates by the principle "nothing ventured, nothing lost." Perfectionism is another destructive trait. For some good students, their solid achievements are "not good enough," they should have done better. There are talented students in prestigious colleges who feel they don't belong there, that their acceptance was a "fluke." They are not aware that many of their classmates feel the same way.

Incidentally, the first year of college, especially away from home, may be enormously stressful. There are so many problems: adapting to a dorm, a new roommate, new classmates, new methods of teaching, the lack of family supervision, and so on. Freedom is wonderful, but so many don't know how to handle it. Not all 18 year olds are ready to go away to college.

Sex and Marriage

Probably more patients come into therapy because of problems with sex and marriage (or divorce) than for any other reason.

Many patients have difficulty talking about sex. It is an intensely personal subject and they resent prying, even by a therapist. The topic is embarrassing and regularly accompanied by feelings of guilt, especially about fantasies and impulses. It is probably best to ask a general question about sex as part of life history and see how the patient responds. If the patient is hesitant, then go on to other topics. There will be opportunities to explore it further in the course of later discussions of relationships and marriage.

It should be mentioned that not all the difficulties in getting a history of sexual activities are due to the patient, some are contributed by the therapist. Many therapists are embarrassed by the topic and this communicates itself to the patient. And there are also therapists who are not free of voyeuristic impulses and dwell on the topic excessively, to the detriment of the course of therapy.

Mention also should be made of uninhibited patients who describe their sexual adventures in lurid detail. This behavior is more frequent with borderline personalities. They often are being seductive, consciously or unconsciously. Therapists are human beings and will respond to erotic material. Needless to say, if it threatens the course of therapy, it needs to be analyzed and resolved. Sometimes the therapist himself needs to consult a colleague to keep the therapy from foundering.

Problems with marriage and divorce bring many into seeking help. This is too big an area to discuss here except to caution the therapist not to take sides or give premature advice until the issues are explored carefully.

Previous Therapy

It was mentioned in the previous chapter, but it deserves further attention. If the patient was in treatment previously, this needs to be explored. If the patient was helped, the new therapist has a significant advantage. The patient will trust more readily and is hopeful about being helped again. If the previous therapy was unsuccessful, then the new therapist is forewarned. She should try to find out what went wrong and, if possible, not repeat it.

PITFALLS

The therapist is responsible for conducting the therapy and is responsible for dealing with everything the patient said, and left unsaid. The narrative that even well-motivated patients tell is not entirely true and complete. It is a personalized account of what happened and has gaps and distortions. Some events are left out entirely, others are altered. In the course of therapy, with a better relationship and benefiting from free associations and recall of repressed material, the history becomes more complete and accurate.

Patients may consciously avoid bringing up certain events or they have repressed them and are not even aware of them. Certain periods are too painful. Patients do not like to appear stupid and may leave out other actions which may portray them in a bad light. Also, patients may avoid some periods of their history and come to feel that if they don't talk about it, they do not have to assume responsibility for it. The capacity for self-deception is enormous.

The therapist is responsible for what has been left out, or implied, as well as what was said explicitly. She knows that the story is not complete and needs to be alert to recognize the gaps. If the patient complains bitterly, and at length about his mother, the alert therapist wonders "where was the father when all this was going on." Even the best motivated patients who are trying to be completely honest leave gaps. Patients who deliberately lie are most difficult to treat.

PRACTICAL SUGGESTIONS

These are some suggestions that may be of help. The author has found it useful to construct a chart with the names and ages of the significant others in the patient's life and the anniversaries of important events. Therapists usually have good memories, but they can't remember everything. If the case load includes many patients who come at infrequent intervals, it is easy to forget details. It is embarrassing to forget the name of the wife, or how many children and so on, with a patient who has been coming for a long time. In the interval between patients, it is useful to take a quick look on the chart before you greet the next patient. Therapists don't have to have perfect memories.

How do you remember everything you tell patients? It is not always possible, but good notes help. Another strategy that I use is: does it sound like me?

Clinical Illustration:

Patient: "I'm going to divorce my husband, as you advised."
Me: "Did I say that? It doesn't sound like me."
Patient: "Oh, you said he was not likely to change."

There is still another complication in history-taking. Some events are so vivid in patients' memories that they are sure they told you about them, but they haven't. They may insist that they did tell you. Don't argue with them; simply state that you think you would have remembered, if they had.

Another practice of mine that may be useful: If I decide that I will take the person as a regular patient, I don't do a formal *mental status examination*, unless I need it for a report. The mental status puts the therapist in the role of examiner and the patient becomes the examinee. It interferes with the development of the spirit of collaboration that is best for therapy. Furthermore, within a few sessions, the patient probably reveals all the affective and cognitive data that would be obtained by the regular mental status examination.

Chapter 4

EARLY PHASES OF TREATMENT

The therapist is faced with important decisions. Based on the information she has obtained from the initial interview, the life history and her impression of the patient, she has to decide where to begin and how to begin. The plan for treatment should be flexible since she is continuing to learn more about the patient.

Some patients who come into treatment are beginning to fall apart. They need to be patched up, held together and their suffering relieved to some extent before anything else can be done. They need support, reassurance and advice. Do not analyze, do not stir things up.

And then there are patients who have a well-functioning character structure but have a problem for which they have decided to get professional help. From their history you know that they have coped successfully with many challenges in their careers and personal lives. With such patients you can start interpreting from the very beginning.

Most patients will be somewhere in between, and the therapist will need to be flexible and tailor the therapy to the changing needs of the patient. The great majority of patients will need varying degrees of guidance and support.

The emphasis in the early sessions is on helping the patient to express himself more freely and building the relationship. You want the patient to express all his feelings, thoughts, memories, dreams and fantasies as completely and honestly as possible. This is hard for most people. The classic analytic instruction to the patient is: "Say everything that comes to mind, it's all important. Try not to censor anything." This was to encourage free association. This is still a useful way to start, and some patients will do well with it. Most patients need more guidance.

Many patients will run out of things to say after a few hours. They are not sure what's important, what you want from them. People want freedom but most don't know what to do with it. They've never before had a conversation like this. Usually they talk to someone about whom they know a great deal, and who shares in the conversation. Rarely has anyone said: "Tell me all about yourself." This is a new experience, and they need time to adjust as well as guidelines.

As long as the patient is productive, don't do anything much more than listen carefully and ask an occasional question to clarify some point. An occasional smile and nodding of the head is also good. Do not feel that you have to make interpretations, solve problems or give advice before you are ready. Don't allow yourself to be rushed. The patient is getting a great deal of implicit support by being able to talk about his problems freely to an attentive listener. Many therapists are concerned about *doing* something for the patient, but the essence of treatment is *being* with the patient.

In the early sessions, don't permit long periods of silence especially when the patient appears uncomfortable with them. This is the time to ask questions about topics which are not too disturbing. Usually questions about interpersonal relations are a safe area; patients find it easier to talk about others than themselves.

Where to Start

Another early decision is where to start. Most often, we follow the patient's lead and start with the problem which brought him into therapy. It may be obvious that a more basic conflict exists, but the patient may not be ready to talk about it. Also, the patient may become impatient with a therapist who goes into great detail about events in childhood when they are concerned with a pressing current problem. As a general rule, it is better to wait until a good working alliance has been established before tackling some of the thornier issues. Many topics that are best avoided early can be successfully dealt with later on.

There are exceptions to all rules. A patient may present with a stormy marital problem, but the history indicates that, although she doesn't consider herself an alcoholic, she does have a serious drinking problem. With tact, the therapist may steer her into dealing with this problem first with great benefit to the patient. Also, in brief therapy because of the constraints of time, the therapist may say that the presenting problem is not nearly as significant as some other and suggest that they start with that. The patient may go along, and then again she may not.

Early Moves

You are still trying to get a more complete picture of this person. A safe assumption is that there is much more to him (or her) than you have learned in two or three hours. What has been left out of the narrative? If the patient talks mainly about her husband, what about the children, her mother, other family and friends? If the patient continues to talk only about the past, try to steer him to the present. And vice-versa. If the patient tends to speak about general topics, ask specific questions (*"can you give me an example?"*). If the patient concentrates on minute details, try to expand the discussion ("where else does it happen?", "any idea why it seems to happen so often?", "do you have a theory about it?").

We try to identify the individual's liabilities and what difficulties they cause. We also try to identify the assets of the individual and the successes achieved. Most patients tend to take their successes for granted and focus on their failures. They are not "good enough," they "should have" done better. An objective of therapy is to help the patient gain a better perspective. We tend to focus too much on the problems and not enough on the strengths of the patient.

We also try to get a clear picture of how this person has dealt with his anxieties and managed to survive all these years. What strategies has she used to get along with people? Was the patient predominantly compliant? This is the most common pattern of relating. They "get along because they go along." He wants to please people and is quick to agree with others. Above all, he wants approval and acceptance, he wants everybody to be his friend. It is hard for him to compete or confront others. He is a follower, not a leader; he is more comfortable as an employee rather than the boss. Criticism and rejection are very painful, and he tries hard to avoid them. He needs everyone to like /love him.

Quite different in behavior are the predominantly aggressive personalities. They see the world as a jungle, where everyone is a potential enemy and only a fool goes around trusting others to do the right thing. They are confident of their own abilities and feel superior to others. They are fighters and good competitors; criticism doesn't bother them too much. People don't have to like them; they'd rather that others admire, respect/fear them.

And then there are those who are predominantly detached. They try to keep their contacts with the world to a minimum. They do not fully employ their talents and abilities, often doing without rather than putting up with the hassles necessary to acquire things. Above all, they value privacy and personal freedom.

These brief outlines are not meant to be complete descriptions of character structures, only to illustrate the process of observing and learning about patients. We also want to note the changes over the years. The obedient child may become a rebellious adolescent and still later the conforming adult. Or the patient may seem stuck in the mode of the rebellious adolescent all his life. And the "baby in the family" may always remain a baby.

Obviously, there is much to learn about this individual in order to help him. We need to evaluate his anxieties and depressions, and his neurotic defenses, when they work and when they don't. To the extent that people are neurotic, they go to extremes, they don't know when to stop. Instead of learning from experience, they repeat their mistakes again and again.

Overcoming Alienation

Another important trait in the neurotic is that they are not in good contact with their feelings. This is called alienation, from the word alien; the person is a stranger to himself. An important goal in therapy is to counter this alienation. In discussing an event, always ask the patient: "and how did you *feel* when that happened?" Many patients have trouble answering, often giving intellectual answers. The therapist needs to persist and ask about feelings. In dreams, an important aspect is the mood of the dream. In time, the patient learns the valuable lesson: feelings are more important than ideas.

Alienation manifests itself by boredom, feelings of emptiness and, when severe, by feelings of deadness. In the most severe form, it results in amnesia, the person doesn't even know his name. There is a novel by Albert Camus, appropriately entitled "The Stranger" which gives an excellent portrayal of the life-style of a severely alienated man.

Educating the Patient

Most patients need help in learning how to be a patient and how to collaborate with the therapist. It is not enough to tell them "say everything that comes to mind." We ask them to speak freely, to hold judgment in abeyance, and not to suppress painful or conflictful material. What they could not face alone, they now may be able to face with the help of the therapist.

Many patients live disorganized or "scattered" lives, and therapy furnishes an opportunity to help them develop some structure in their daily routine. Their appointed "hour" is their responsibility; if they miss it, they still pay for it. If they are 10 minutes late, their session is 10 minutes shorter. Sessions start on time and end on time. If the patient has little to say for most of the session and begins to bring up significant material in the last few minutes, *do not run past the hour.* Simply say that this is important data and to bring it up at the next meeting. If the patient gets angry, then you have a very significant issue to discuss.

A related issue is: telephone calls from patients. Some patients will phone several times during the week but have little to say during the session. Needless to say, this is not good. Some therapists want no phone calls but want all discussion to take place during the scheduled meetings. They feel that phone calls are an imposition. Furthermore, they interfere with therapy; the therapist cannot adequately deal with important issues in a few minutes at all hours of the day or night.

Other therapists may have a more flexible policy. They will accept phone calls early in therapy and gradually wean the patients away from the practice. Some therapists never give out their home number. With a few patients, I have given them my home phone number (or where I will be on vacation), and they have rarely called except for valid emergencies. It was enough for them that they could call if they needed to.

Dealing with Resistance

Indications that therapy is not going well are such events as: patient has nothing to say ("my mind is a blank"), coming late to sessions, complaints about fees (especially when they seem to have money for everything else), expressing doubts about the efficacy of treatment, questions about your competence, and so on. The time-tested rule of thumb is: *go along while the transference is positive, but intervene when it turns negative.* Resistances need to be dealt with actively or therapy may come to a premature halt.

Some Illustrations:

1. Patient: "I feel like a bump on a log. I have nothing to say, all talked out."
Therapist: "This is not easy. A human being is not a tape recorder. You can't turn it on, continue for 45 minutes and then stop. If you could talk, you would. Silence can also be valuable, a time to reflect."

2. Patient: "I don't feel we are getting anywhere, just re-hashing the same old stuff."
Therapist: "These are difficult problems with which you have struggled for a long time. If they were easy, you would have solved them a long time ago. I don't feel that we know fully what is going on. *From my experience, I believe that, in time, we can come up with something better than what we have now.*"
(Comment: The therapist was indicating that he successfully dealt with such problems before. It was appropriate reassurance.)

3. Patient: "How the hell is talking going to help me?"
Therapist: "It's not talking that helps so much, it's listening. You learn by listening to yourself, as well as to what I have to say about some of your problems."

The most serious threats to therapy come from transference and countertransference. These will be dealt with in greater detail in a later chapter.

Aims of Therapy

The aims of therapy are not only to relieve, or eliminate, troublesome symptoms but also to help the patient develop better interpersonal relationships and to be more productive. The important things in life, according to Freud, are: "Love and work." We want to help the patient more fully develop his talents, gain a measure of self-respect and perhaps a greater capacity for enjoyment. We try to help the patient grow.

These are ambitious objectives. Most patients can make substantial progress toward these goals if they persevere. The process is sometimes painful, but also stimulating and, at times, exhilarating.

The helping process began when the patient first decided that she was not happy with her existence and that perhaps she could do something about it. We want to encourage these early, tentative steps in the formidable task of really understanding one's self. Dynamic psychotherapy is a process of "working toward increasing awareness, taking place in a matrix of unique, evolving human relationship."

Chapter 5

INTERPRETATION AND INSIGHT

All therapies provide support (explicit and implicit), advice, counseling and information. The unique feature of dynamic therapy is that it has as a major goal, the development of insight. For this reason, it is also called insight-oriented therapy.

Insight is a word in common usage and means perception, understanding and discernment. In therapy, its special meaning is that it attempts to provide understanding of material of which the individual previously was unaware. It is making conscious what was formerly unconscious. The classic analytic formulation is: "where id was, there ego shall be."

The development of insight means that the individual now has a better understanding of his feelings and behavior. This is not only an intellectual awareness, but a fuller understanding of all aspects of the problem, especially of the emotional aspects. There are different levels of knowledge. We may know about certain things in a general or theoretical way, enough to recognize it and to be able to categorize it. And then there is knowledge of all aspects of a problem so that we feel we have mastered it. This is the kind of insight we try to achieve in therapy. The individual may now be able to resolve some conflicts which he never could before. Now, he may be free enough to try some alternative approaches and deal more successfully with certain situations. Insight leads to growth.

The therapist encourages the development of insight by means of interpretation. Interpretation includes questions, comments, suggestions, and gestures. The aim of these technical maneuvers is to call the patient's attention to an existing problem or to suggest possible meanings to what he is thinking, feeling or doing.

Interpretations may consist of interrupting the patient's flow of words with a simple "Oh!" or "Hmm." To the perceptive patient, that means what she has just said bears looking into a little more closely. Repeating what the patient has just said, in the patient's words, is a forceful confrontation indicating that what the patient just described has greater significance than he apparently ascribes to it. Not laughing at a joke that the patient just told is also an interpretation. Not answering a question of the patient is also an intervention which may lead to insight. Patients usually get angry when the therapist does not answer a question, but it also gets them thinking. There is an old saying: "No answer is also an answer."

Clinical Illustrations:

1. The patient described some inept or stupid action and then said, without much feeling: "Boy, am I a jerk!"
Therapist: "Yes, you are a jerk." Using his very own words, the therapist forcefully brought home to him the significance of his behavior which he was accustomed to treating so casually. Such confrontations are potent and should be used with discretion.

2. Patient: (feeling abused) "Can you imagine a wife talking to her husband like that?"
Therapist "Yes, I can."

3. Clinical Example: This was a physician with many phobias whose wife had to accompany him wherever he went. In a bragging tone, he mentioned that he always got to his office on time to see his patients.
Patient: "That's the least I can do."
Therapist: "That's the most you can do; you do little else."

Almost all patients require preparation to help them achieve insight. The therapist does this by stimulating the patient's interest with such questions as: "where else does it happen?", "how did you feel about it?", what did you do then?", "what else comes to mind?". We try to get associations. We can also call attention to a topic by summarizing the data we have thus far. It's best to use the patient's own words, but we need to be sure that we know what he or she means by them.

These stimulating comments usually are well tolerated by patients who are encouraged to explore the issues further. The more the patient does on his own, the better. We try not to tell him directly, but guide him to find out for himself.

There are also revealing interpretations which deal with topics the patient has so far avoided or denied. These are often very traumatic and to be used cautiously. We try not to confront the patient with insight which he cannot tolerate. Some examples are: "I don't think your husband is going to change any time soon. He's an alcoholic but continues to deny it." Or, "Your son's behavior suggests that he's gay."

Timing of Interpretation

We try to time revealing interpretations when the patient is close to making it herself or indicates some readiness to cope with this new reality. The timing of interpretation is far from an exact science. With experience, therapists develop their judgment about how fast to move with a particular patient, avoiding the extremes of premature interpretation or of waiting too long.

Some Guidelines

Interpretations that may jar the patient are best made when the therapy and events in the life of the patient are proceeding smoothly. Leave enough time for discussion and ventilation. They should not be made when the session is about to end. Don't make them just before the patient (or therapist) is going on vacation. If the interpretation was premature and the patient becomes angry, don't argue, just listen. The best defense for the therapist is no defense. Just listen and don't interrupt. Another rule of thumb: *when in doubt about making an interpretation, don't.*

Working Through

One interpretation is not likely to lead to a change in a characteristic trait or enduring change in behavior. It requires repetition before a new pattern of behavior or attitude is established. Initial improvement after an interpretation is encouraging, but there is a danger of backsliding. The new insight is repeated, whenever the opportunity presents, in the varying contexts in which it appears. This "working through" requires time and persistence.

Clinical Illustrations

> 1. The patient is a successful stockbroker in his 40's who came into therapy for a depressive episode. In one session, he mentioned an argument with his wife who berated him for forgetting her birthday. He tried to make light of his lapse and attributed it to the pressures at work. In an earlier session, he stated that "he loved his wife and had been happily married for 15 years."

The therapist has several options, he can say: "Forgetting your wife's birthday shows hostility." The patient would likely reject this interpretation and protest that he "loved" her. Another option for the therapist would be: "Tell me about your wife; we haven't talked much about her." This would encourage the patient to give a more complete picture of his wife and the relationship. While he believes he "loves" his wife, the discussion reveals there are areas of serious disagreement about their life-style. He is much more ambitious than she is: he would like a larger house, send the children to private school, she doesn't entertain enough, etc. In the course of the discussion, he begins to realize that at times he has been very angry with her. For the most part, the anger has been denied and not expressed. The latter approach by the therapist is much more productive and may lead to insight about the marriage which he can accept.

> 2. The patient finds a letter to a friend that he was sure he mailed, but apparently "forgot." This was not like him. The therapist could say: "You didn't want to send it." This may be a valid interpretation, but it misses an opportunity to find out more. The therapist could also say: "Tell me about the letter," or, "Tell me about your friend." The patient then elaborates that this is a friend of many years, a man whom he likes and respects. However, the man is going into a new venture and wants the patient to invest in it. The patient has trouble refusing this friend but also feels it would be a bad investment. In the letter, he makes up several excuses why he can't invest at this time. He was not happy with the letter.

This latter approach is far more productive for the course of therapy. The patient was in conflict and was not happy with the action he took. This is an important area to explore. The first interpretation was not wrong, but the second was better.

Evaluating Interpretations

How can we evaluate the effectiveness of our interpretations? The patient may explicitly corroborate the interpretation and add confirmatory material. The patient may also feel better: less tense, a feeling of relief, and a physical symptom (headache or fatigue) may diminish. Or the patient may confirm it implicitly by the nature of his next association which keeps moving the therapy forward. A not very reliable guide is the feeling that the interpretation "clicks." This may, or may not, be confirmed by subsequent events.

Of course, in time, the most valid criterion is that the new insight is reflected by constructive changes in the patient's life and environment. A considerable period of time may elapse before this becomes apparent.

IN SUMMARY

Interpretation is a fundamental process in dynamic psychotherapy. What was unconscious was made conscious. The patient now understands something that he was doing of which he was previously unaware. What he didn't know was hurting him. He repressed this out of awareness because he didn't know how to deal with it. Uncovering is difficult and usually painful. Timing is important and patients need to be prepared to cope with the new reality. Supported by the relationship with the therapist, and using her resources more effectively, the patient is able to face issues that she formerly avoided or repressed.

Chapter 6

USE OF DREAMS

Dreams are of the greatest importance in understanding a person. In a dream we are talking to ourselves but in a language that requires translation. It is distorted by the use of symbols, condensation, displacement and repression. The dream does not respect time, logic or reality; here nothing is impossible. The dream is a creative production similar to a play; the dreamer is the playwright and the setting, actors and plot are whatever her/his imagination can create.

For centuries, poets and philosophers recognized that dreams were significant, but their understanding was intuitive and without a scientific frame of reference. The systematic study of dreams began with Sigmund Freud who considered the "Interpretation of Dreams" his greatest work. He was a good dreamer. According to Freud, dreams represent the fulfillment of a repressed infantile wish. The wish is not acceptable, consciously, and therefore appears in a disguised, symbolic form in order to preserve sleep and not disturb the dreamer. It is a compromise between the ego and instincts. Abstract ideas are transformed into images and the content is expressed in action. Freud felt that dreams were "the royal road to the unconscious."

Like many of the neo-Freudians (Walter Bonime, Eric Fromm, Montague Ullman and many others), Karen Horney felt that to concentrate on the wish-fulfillment in dreams was not to do justice to the rich material that dreams made accessible. She felt that dreams afford us a glimpse into the private world of the dreamer where he is in better contact with his real self. Awake, we share a public world with all the limitations imposed by reality; asleep, we are in our own private realm. Nothing is as intimate as a dream. When awake, consciousness is restricted to cope with all the realistic demands; asleep, our awareness expands and we are in better contact with our feelings. A depression may manifest itself in dreams, weeks or months before the individual becomes consciously aware of it. Dreams express underlying conflicts but also the personal resources available for constructive solution of problems. Real problems have been solved in the course of dreaming. Most students of the subject recognize that dreams are meaningful expressions of the person's struggle for self-realization.

GENERAL CONSIDERATIONS

What we remember of the dream is the "manifest dream," not the complete, original dream. In gaining access to consciousness, many details are lost and only fragments may remain. In the process of waking up, some material may be added to make the dream more coherent or logical. This process, called secondary elaboration, also makes the interpretation of dreams more difficult. Many events are condensed, displaced or blended into a composite.

And of course, much is expressed in symbols. We ask the dreamer to free-associate to the various parts of the dream in order to get a more complete picture and to try to understand what the symbols mean. This "dream work" results in an expanded dream which now includes some of the "latent" content. Many authorities feel that latent content is the much more significant part of the dream. Other authorities now feel that the manifest dream has been relatively neglected and is very significant in its own right.

There is no uniformity of opinion on symbols. Freud believed symbols were universal, they represented the same thing for everyone. Others feel that symbols are personal and may represent different things to different individuals. For example, a snake may represent evil, deceit, sin, sex or knowledge. The meanings become clear only by the associations of the dreamer. In a person who has a pet snake, a dream about a snake probably will have an idiosyncratic meaning. However, individuals with similar backgrounds will share many symbols which are common to that culture.

Many symbols are puzzling, but some are relatively easy to decipher. Finding one's passport, finding something that has been lost, choosing one path at a crossroads and reaching home, represent constructive actions. The same is true of helping a child, or love for a child. The child, of course, is the dreamer. Everything in the dream relates to the dreamer. It is his dream, he cannot dream anyone else's dream. Usually, sex acts in dreams are not disguised by symbols.

An important element in dreams is the mood. The feelings experienced in the dream are usually accurate reflections of the dreamer's mood. Joy, sadness, fear, anger, sexual feelings are significant elements of the dream. The absence of feeling–"deadness" or "numbness"–is also very significant. A wound that doesn't hurt, or bleed, indicates an individual who is not in good contact with his feelings.

Dreams are useful in treating individuals who are not psychologically sophisticated. The therapist can point out: "these are your dreams, something is going on when you are asleep, maybe they mean something." There are also individuals who shy away from dreams; they come from the mysterious unconscious and cannot be controlled. Such individuals usually are frightened unless they have everything under control.

There are a few patients who bring in such long and detailed dreams that they fill up the entire session. These dreams, of compulsive patients, block therapy because they leave no time to discuss what else is happening. One such dream is enough. If the patient starts another one, stop after one or two minutes and ask about real events in the patient's life. The therapist needs to conduct the course of therapy so that the time will be used effectively.

TECHNIQUE OF INTERPRETATION

The dreamer interprets his own dream, with help. The therapist may ask such questions as:

"Anything come to mind about the dream?", or

"Anything familiar in the dream?", or

"Anything in the dream remind you of a past event or of a particular person?", or

"Anything impress you or appear especially strange in the dream?".

Usually the questions elicit associations which lead to a larger and more accurate portrait of the patient. If none of these questions are productive, you may then say: "Let's leave the dream and go on." The topic the patient may next start talking about is often relevant to the dream. Everything said in that session after a dream is also an association to the dream.

No dream is ever completely interpreted, and there is not only one exactly right interpretation. We try to get as much material as we can from the dream, but it is rare to exhaust all the possibilities. There may be several plausible interpretations, all tell us something significant about the dreamer.

We try for as much spontaneity as possible and don't pressure the patient to bring in dreams. At the time of the initial interview when we ask about sleep patterns, we may ask about dreaming. If the patient asks whether we think dreams are important, we say "definitely yes." As long as the patient is talking about material that gives us a more complete picture, we listen. When the patient runs out of things to say or begins to discuss trivialities, that is a good time to ask whether he remembers any dreams.

We note when the patient brings up the dream. Does she start the session with the dream? In the course of interpretation, we ask about events that occurred the day before the dream ("the day's residue") or during the previous session. If the dream comes up in the middle of the session, what was she talking about just before she remembered the dream?

If the patient brings up the dream just a few minutes before the end of the session, she may be running away, afraid to find out what it means, or is testing to see if you will give her extra time. Almost always, keep the sessions to the time allotted. You may say: "the dream is too important to rush through; please bring it up at the next meeting." It is then important to note whether she does or not. If the patient does bring it up, it is a good sign that the patient is seriously involved in therapy and is trying to maintain continuity. If the patient does not, this confirms that the patient was not ready to explore what the dream meant. We may bring this point up later when it is appropriate ("you didn't say anything about the dream from the last session").

DREAMS OF SPECIAL INTEREST

The First Dream

The first dream is unusually significant and reveals important aspects of the patient and how he approaches therapy. However, unless we know a great deal about the person, we need to be very cautious in our interpretation. We may simply say: "What do you think the dream means?" and let it drop after the patient makes some comment.

Example No. 1:

The patient dreams she is "talking on the phone to someone in a distant city and has a hard time hearing what is being said." Don't interpret, but you can expect the patient will have difficulty with communicating in therapy. If the patient asks you to comment, a safe thing to say is:

"I think the dream is about communication."

Example No. 2:

The patient dreams that he comes into your office and you get up and say: "I'm Dr. Greenberg; I'm an Italian." The patient feels confused. It is safe to assume that "Italian," or some association to Italian, has significance for this patient. Whether you try to find associations to it then or wait until some later time depends on your judgment as to how ready the patient is to go on. We can assume that he probably will make a good patient because in the dream, he is actually in the office talking to the therapist. By contrast, in the first dream the patient was at a great distance from the other person and had a problem with communication.

Anxiety Dreams

Dreams with a lot of anxiety which disturb sleep appear not to fit in with Freud's thesis that they are wish fulfillments and do not disturb sleep. The usual explanation is that the repressed wish is too strong and threatens to break though the censorship. Such dreams are common in posttraumatic stress disorder where the same or a similar dream recurs again and again. These dreams indicate that the individual is still struggling to resolve a conflict. As the patient gets better, the dreams change, become less frequent, less violent and less disturbing.

Anxiety provoking dreams usually include some danger and some impairment with the patient's ability to cope. For example, the patient is being chased by a menacing crowd and he cannot run well, his legs are so heavy that he can barely move them. We try to clarify: what is the danger, what will happen if they catch him, and why can't he run well?

Dreams in the Same Night

When several dreams occur during the same night, we may assume that they have to do with one theme. Even though they appear separate and distinct, we should try to find a common denominator. And if we can, we may learn a great deal about all of them.

Recurring Dreams

The same, or similar, dreams that keep recurring over a long period of time represent a conflict or problem that the patient cannot resolve. They may recur over months or years and are often disturbing and frustrating. In post traumatic stress disorder, the setting is often a scene of danger and the patient does something wrong or fails to do something. The feelings are intense: fear, guilt or horror. Other repetitive dreams involve wandering around, losing one's way, appliances that don't work.

When the individual is making progress to resolve the problem, the dreams become less frequent and then finally stop when he has essentially resolved the conflict.

Transference in Dreams

In all dreams, we need to be alert to pick up clues regarding transference. Do any of the actors in the dream resemble the parents? Do any of them have some of the attributes of the therapist? We may ask the patient: "Could that character in the dream be me?"

Most patients have difficulty in talking about the therapist, especially early in the course of treatment. It is much easier to talk about others, and even about himself, rather than about the therapist. We shall discuss transference in greater detail in a later chapter, but dreams give valuable data about transference long before the patient is able to express them face to face. It is important in the conduct of therapy to know what the patient is feeling. Hostility to the therapist may derail the treatment even before the patient really knows what happened.

Erotic feelings for the therapist, also, may create problems that need to be analyzed and resolved. Knowing what the patient is feeling, as early as possible, is of the greatest help to the therapist in guiding the treatment to a successful conclusion.

Turning-Point Dreams

Some dreams tell us that the patient has made good progress and has now reached a point that bodes well for the future. These have been called "turning-point" dreams.

Clinical Example:

This was a young man, now in his third year of once a week therapy. He started this session with the following dream:

> I was the only passenger in a car that was going fast over winding roads. The road was familiar. No one was in the driver's seat and I was frightened. After a time, I moved into the driver's seat and took the wheel. I could steer, but the brakes didn't work. Finally, I shifted into a lower gear and the car slowed down.

The patient said: "I don't need help interpreting this dream." In many previous dreams, the patient had always been a passenger, passively riding in a bus or car. In this dream, for the first time, he moved into the driver's seat and had some control of the vehicle. He still had serious problems, but made good progress and functioned very much better in his profession and in his personal life.

Written Dreams

Some patients dream frequently but can't remember them. They may ask if they should write them down. Since much of the value of dream interpretation depends on associations to the various parts, a written dream that the patient has largely forgotten will reveal little. To a new patient, I would say: "Don't write them down; in time you'll remember them."

After a period of time, if the patient has not remembered any dream, I would suggest that he could write them down. When he brings in a written dream, I would ask him for the notes and ask what he remembers of the dream without consulting his notes. The discrepancy between the oral and written versions may be significant.

DREAM APPRECIATION

Montague Ullman and coworkers have done interesting work with exploration of dreams by a group of patients. Instead of dream interpretation, they call their efforts "dream appreciation." The term indicates that they set high value on, and appreciate, the creative process involved in dreaming. Instead of spending most of the time in deciphering the symbols, they concentrate on the behavior of the dreamer. They encourage each patient to become his, or her, own authority in dream analysis.

SUMMING UP

In a dream, you are talking to yourself. Nothing is as intimate as a dream; the dreamer is in much closer contact with his feelings than when awake. With help from the therapist, the patient interprets his own dream. In all dreams we look for allusions to the transference. It is more important to understand the dreamer than to interpret all the symbols in the dream. There is no one correct interpretation and rarely is any dream completely interpreted.

SUGGESTIONS FOR FURTHER READING

1. Kuper, A., & Stone, A.: The dream of Irma's injection: A structural analysis. *American Journal of Psychiatry* 1982; 139: 1225-1239.
2. Bonime, W.: *The Clinical Use of Dreams.* DaCapo Press, New York, 1982.
3. Ullman, M., & Zimmerman, N.: *Working with Dreams.* Delacorte Press, New York, 1979.

Chapter 7

THERAPIST-PATIENT RELATIONSHIP:
TRANSFERENCE, COUNTERTRANSFERENCE
AND THE WORKING ALLIANCE

Many authorities believe that Freud's discovery of transference was his major contribution to the technique of analytic therapy. The feelings of the patient for the therapist, which so often block treatment, are also the key to understanding the most important character traits of the patient. Transference reactions give us a valuable opportunity to explore the patient's past experiences and how they continue to influence his behavior in the present. How the patient behaves in the office is also how he behaves in the outside world.

The following anecdote about Freud comes from a reliable source, and even if it never happened, it sheds valuable light on transference reactions:

> As she was leaving the office at the end of a session, the patient said to Freud: "Professor, you really are a handsome man." After showing her out, Freud looked in the mirror. The next patient was also a woman, and as she left at the end of the session, she turned to him and said: "Freud, you really are an ugly man." Again Freud looked in the mirror and could see no change in his appearance from the previous hour.

DEFINITION OF TRANSFERENCE

The term means that the individual displaces or "transfers" attitudes that have developed in the past into the present. The person misinterprets the present in terms of his past. It is largely an unconscious process, and the individual is not aware that in this current situation his attitudes, feelings, ideas, fears and fantasies are a carry-over from the past. They may not be appropriate to present circumstances.

The term transference was first used only to refer to the process in analysis when the attitudes and feelings that had developed in childhood in relation to the parents, now were displaced onto the analyst. This was the intraanalytic transference. One of the important reasons for keeping the analyst relatively anonymous was that it facilitated the transference. Analysis of transference became one of the key processes in analytic therapy. In time, it was recognized that the phenomena of transference were not limited to the relationship between patient and analyst, but were universal. It operates in all human relationships, and to the extent that people are neurotic, the perceptions of those we relate to are distorted to a greater or lesser extent. Instead of a relationship that involves a subject and an object, in a transference reaction we have the subject relating simultaneously to a present object and a past object.

POSITIVE AND NEGATIVE TRANSFERENCE

Positive transference is the term used to designate the relationship when the patient's feelings toward the therapist are predominantly friendly, trusting, admiring, respectful and loving. With positive transference, it is much easier for the patient to express herself or himself. Positive transference makes it easier for the early phase of therapy to get underway and need not be analyzed until treatment is well-established. We need to mention that, at times, a "positive" transference can become so intense that it blocks treatment and acts as a "negative" transference. Instances of this are when the patient "falls madly in love" with the therapist and talks of nothing else but her feelings for the therapist. Of course, this needs to be analyzed without delay.

Negative transference refers to the relationship when the patient dislikes, mistrusts or hates the therapist. It manifests itself by anger, hostility and various resistances to therapy: having little to say during the sessions, coming late, objecting to fees, challenging the value of therapy or the competence of the therapist, making demands for special consideration, cancelling appointments capriciously, and so on. Negative transference needs to be dealt with when it appears, or therapy may end prematurely. Probably the most common cause of poor results in psychotherapy is failure to analyze negative transference reactions.

The rule of thumb: in the beginning, as long as the patient is cooperative, keeps her appointments and talks about significant events, don't analyze the transference. Don't interrupt as long as you continue to learn more about the patient's life and problems. However, when negative transference reactions appear, they do need to be analyzed or treatment may come to an abrupt halt.

ANALYZING TRANSFERENCE REACTIONS

In classical analysis which went on for many months, and years, the therapist could wait patiently, and passively, until a great deal of material emerged about early childhood and unambiguous maternal or paternal transference reactions were expressed. These were then interpreted. The analyst made fewer mistakes but much time was wasted. Therapists were not alert to transference in the here and now, and those occurring in extraanalytic situations. As a result, treatment was excessively prolonged, and analyses were often felt to be "interminable."

In current practice, especially with the focus on object relations, therapists are much more active and aware of transference reactions. The quality of therapy, therefore, is better and much less time is wasted. There is a risk, however, that the attempt to move the therapy along faster will lead to premature interpretations.

COUNTERTRANSFERENCE

Countertransference is a transference reaction of a therapist to the patient. It is a parallel to the transference, but going in the opposite direction. The therapist is not approaching the patient with an open mind, without prejudice, but reacting as though the patient were a significant figure in the therapist's life. For example: the therapist may "confuse" his adolescent patient with his own adolescent son and not be fully aware that this is happening. A major goal of analysis or therapy for the therapist, as part of his professional training, is to uncover and resolve these neurotic conflicts so that they do not interfere with the conduct of therapy. Therapists are not entirely free of neurotic traits.

Therapists may be more comfortable with some patients than with others. They may dislike homosexuals, domineering women, very wealthy men, certain ethnic groups, and so on. You do not have to like all your patients, but if there is a strong feeling of antipathy, you need to understand its source or it will interfere with successful treatment. Also, if there is very great attraction to a patient, the therapist may find it hard to be objective. I know of one prominent psychiatrist who has mentioned to colleagues that on a few occasions patients who were referred to him were so attractive that he knew he couldn't listen to them objectively, and he therefore referred them to others.

It is a mistake to assume that all neurotic traits reside in the patient and that the therapist is totally free of them. It is not that simple. Usually the patient does have the preponderance of neurotic traits, but therapists are not entirely free of them. Some therapists have great difficulty in admitting that they ever made a mistake, and that the patient was right. This is a reversal of roles and makes them uncomfortable. They may misinterpret countertransference for transference, e.g. the therapist may feel that the patient is hostile when, in fact, he is the one who is angry at the patient.

We often learn more from our mistakes than from our successes. Those therapists who can admit mistakes may learn a great deal from their patients. In the close relationship of therapy, the patient is also observing the therapist and, in time, may get to know her very well. Comments of the patients about the therapist are frequently very insightful. One of the benefits of experience to the therapist is that she or he has learned a great deal from patients. One of my teachers was fond of saying: "Your patients will not only pay you, they will help you."

THE WORKING ALLIANCE

An important component of the therapist-patient relationship is the working alliance. This is the relatively nonneurotic rapport that usually develops between people who are working together. The patient is seeking relief from symptoms, and the therapist has a serious interest in understanding the problems and in helping to resolve them. The feelings are predominantly friendly, trusting and rational. Their relationship has similarities to that between teacher and pupil, between colleagues in the same field, and in many other situations. Fundamentally, it is a constructive relationship between two human beings working to achieve a common objective.

The working alliance operates in all forms of psychotherapy: dynamic, cognitive, behavioral, supportive, etc. When therapies are successful, an important role is played by the working alliance. Freud called it the "conscious and unobjectionable" component of transference.

CLINICAL APPLICATIONS

The most common cause of poor results in therapy is failure to deal with the resistance provided by negative transference reactions. Whenever the patient is having trouble speaking freely, suspect transference. Patients often have difficulty talking about the therapist face-to-face. In the beginning, they talk about other people, then about themselves, and last about the therapist. Whenever a patient is having difficulty speaking freely, the therapist should suspect transference. Asking: *"I wonder if you may be having some feelings toward me which are not coming out in the open?"* is often a very successful intervention at resolving the impasse.

Clinical Example

I was working in a different area of the hospital and got to my office 10 minutes late; the patient was in the waiting room. I opened the door and just said: "Hello." This was a patient who usually had a lot to say, but after a few casual remarks, there was a long silence. I then asked: "How did you feel while waiting for me?." With some reluctance he said: "I was very busy today and hurried to get here on time, only to find that you were not in. I was annoyed, no, really angry. Then I thought something important held you up." After some more discussion of his feelings, the rest of the session was very productive.

Comment: This was not planned; I wanted to be on time. If he were a new patient, I would have said: "I'm sorry I'm late." Since he was an old patient, I decided to wait to see what would happen. He was angry but had started to rationalize so he would not have to confront me. Our discussion helped him to express himself and reduce the feelings of resentment. He also found out that it was permissible to criticize the therapist; he was not rejected. He did not have to rationalize or suppress his feelings and could give full attention to his current problems. As a result, the rest of the session was very productive.

Some therapists deliberately provoke anger in patients so they can discuss the problems patients may have with expressing anger. Most therapists, myself included, do not do this and feel that this is staged and contrived. The transference should not be manipulated; there will be enough spontaneous events to analyze if the therapists are alert to these opportunities.

This is an appropriate time to point out that some therapists are intimidated by patients, want to be liked and especially don't want them to get angry. They placate the patients in many ways: adjust appointments, fees, help them with employers, authorities, spouses, and provide extratherapeutic services. They are often not fully aware of what they are doing and rationalize that they are just being helpful. They are susceptible to being manipulated by patients, especially borderline patients. Being "kind" to patients is not always good therapy, and we may miss an opportunity to analyze an important character trait. Also, therapy may come to a premature end when the therapist finally becomes angry at being exploited and refuses to go along with ever more outrageous requests.

We may not always know what the patient is doing, *but therapists should try very hard to know what they are doing, and what they hope to accomplish.*

EROTIC TRANSFERENCE

Case Illustration:

The patient was an attractive young woman coming twice a week for analytically-oriented therapy. At first she was inhibited when talking about her sexual experiences but after a few sessions began describing them in great detail.

The male therapist was excited listening to the adventures of his patient and tried very hard to suppress his feelings. After some self-analysis, the therapist realized that the patient was being seductive. This was transference and a threat to treatment unless dealt with. He began to broaden the discussion so that it went beyond the sexual details and include the relationship with these men. It soon became apparent that the patient was involved with unsuitable people; the relationships were destructive. The patient felt she was demeaning herself. This had been a long-standing pattern. After further elaboration and working through, she began to be more discriminating in her choice of partners. Later, in the course of therapy she would admit that she had been attracted to the therapist. She also realized that he, too, was an inappropriate choice. One result of therapy was that her relations with men improved.

Comment: Listening to a patient is not only an intellectual exercise. The therapist is not just listening to words but to the whole patient, and the reactions to the patient are important clues. In this instance, the therapist correctly analyzed his feelings and helped the patient achieve a very important insight. The therapist became aware that the patient's behavior in the outside world had important transference implications.

Sexual attraction between patient and therapist poses a real hazard, and it is the responsibility of the therapist to see that the ethical boundaries are observed. The temptations may be very great, and, unfortunately, even experienced psychiatrists have not always lived up to professional ethics. The results are great harm to patients and to their own their careers. This topic will be discussed in greater detail in a subsequent chapter.

Too Much Too Soon

While we like therapy to start with a positive attitude, we need to be careful when it seems like it's too good. Some patients are quick with extravagant praise for the therapist and in the first or second session may make remarks like:

"You are just the therapist I have been looking for all these years," "I wish I had heard about you sooner; my previous therapist was a disaster," and so on.

Therapists enjoy hearing such comments, but they are to be treated with caution. This happened too quickly; the patient does not have enough real evidence on which to make this assessment. It is too much, too soon and subject to change quickly. Borderline personalities are especially prone to glorify therapists and then, just as quickly, knock them down. There is no middle ground.

When this happens, an attempt needs to be made to put things in better perspective. The focus should be on what was discussed in the sessions and what was actually accomplished. If some progress was made, that's good, but it doesn't merit extravagant praise. It may also be productive to inquire about how the patient begins other relationships. Do they start with great expectation only to end quickly in disappointment? What the patient does with you, she also does with others in her life.

The opposite also occurs. The patient starts off with a negative attitude and hostility. Usually, it is best to allow the patient to ventilate until the intensity of feelings lessen. Some patients will appreciate that you heard them out, that you listened and didn't interrupt. Don't make interpretations when the patient is very angry, they won't hear you. Wait until they are ready to listen.

Clinical Example:

> This man came in reluctantly; his marriage was stormy and the wife insisted that he see a psychiatrist. His attitude was hostile and skeptical. After a few remarks about his marriage, he launched into a diatribe: he didn't like doctors, they didn't care about patients, only cared about money, expensive homes, vacations, playing golf, etc. etc. Worst of all were the psychiatrists who charged the most and did the least.

When the patient seemed to slow down somewhat, the psychiatrist said quietly: "You really don't know me well enough to say all those things about me." The patient thought for a time and then agreed: "You're right." After that exchange, therapy was quite productive. The patient demonstrated that he could admit that he might be wrong, a valuable asset in therapy.

Avoid Contamination

The conditions under which therapy is conducted make it much easier to recognize transference reactions than in almost any other setting. The therapist is not exactly a "blank screen" but she tries very hard not to intrude her attitudes into the relationship. She listens without judging. She does not react with approval or disapproval to what the patient is saying. She is also a trained observer. The difficulties the patient has in relationships can be seen more clearly in this setting.

It is important that the relationship between patient and therapist not be complicated or blurred. The analytic term for this is "contaminated." If at all possible, it should be kept exclusively between patient and therapist.

If patients ask that their wives (or husbands) come in to explain certain events, *don't permit it.* You can say something like: "It's not necessary, we'll work it out between the two of us." It indicates that you have confidence in the patient, he doesn't need anyone to speak for him. It also avoids many complications.

For the same reason, discourage patients from talking about therapy to friends, except in the most general terms. The opinions of these others will influence the patient; the therapist no longer gets a clear and uncontaminated picture of the patient's thinking and behavior. The same applies to phone calls from friends or relatives of the patient. With rare exceptions, there should be no extensive discussion. Also, the patient should be told who called and what was said.

OBJECT RELATIONS AND SELF PSYCHOLOGY

This is not the book for an adequate discussion of Object Relations and Self Psychology, but since therapists will encounter these terms in the literature, these few remarks may help orient them. Classic Freudian theory is called the drive/structure theory. Many analysts felt that this was not adequate for some patients and developed this alternative theoretical system over the last few decades. The object relational approach emphasizes relationships and probably represents the main stream of the psychoanalytic movement today. The major influence in its development was Heinz Kohut (Kohut 1977), with major contributions from Otto Kernberg (Kernberg 1976).

This theory holds that in order to grow into a mature, competent individual, the person must successfully complete several developmental stages. Failure to do so leaves an emotionally stunted individual. The unmet needs of the patient are reflected in all relationships, including the relationship with the therapist. Transference reactions

are designated as: 1. twinship / kinship
2. idealizing
3. mirroring/ validating.

Object relations psychologists feel that this orientation is very helpful, especially in dealing with narcissistic and borderline personalities. They focus on relationships and tend to be active in the conduct of therapy. There is no consensus, but most authors feel that the theories of Object Relations and Self Psychology are closely interrelated. The reader is advised to consult the extensive literature for an adequate discussion.

SUMMARY

The patient-therapist relationship is the crucial element in successful psychotherapy. Negative transference reactions, unless adequately analyzed, are the most common reason for poor results in psychotherapy. Transference reactions provide the greatest opportunity for insight into the patient's character and how unresolved conflicts from the patient's early life continue to create problems in the present.

RECOMMENDED READING

1. Basch, M.F: *Practicing Psychotherapy.* Basic Books, 1992.
2. Gabbard, G.O.: *Psychodynamic Psychiatry in Clinical Practice.* Washington, D.C., American Psychiatric Press, 1994.
3. Gill M.M.: *Analysis of Transference: Volume I.* New York, International Universities Press, 1982.
4. Kernberg, O.F.: *Object Relations Theory and Clinical Psychoanalysis.* New York, Jason Aronson, 1976.
5. Kohut, H.: *The Restoration of the Self.* New York, International Universities Press, 1977.

Chapter 8

CONDUCTING THERAPY

The therapist conducts the therapy. The therapist is the guide who has been over the terrain before, while for most patients it is a new experience. Diagnosis and treatment go along together in the course of psychotherapy. The therapist formulates a plan to accomplish what she hopes to achieve with this particular patient. The plan has to be tentative, as she continues to learn more about the patient as they go along. She is more objective than the patient. In effect, she is the coach, not the player.

She encourages the patient to speak as freely as he can about his thoughts, feelings, actions, attitudes, prejudices, dreams and fantasies. We try to know everything about the patient: does he put cream in his coffee, what newspapers does he read, and is he afraid to go to the dentist? In this atmosphere of nonjudgmental acceptance, the patient learns that it is safe to speak freely. Except in very unusual circumstances, everything he says will remain confidential. The therapist actively guides the patient to explore areas that may be more rewarding. She also is alert to the gaps in the narrative; what is the patient leaving out? She has no axe to grind, her attitude is "let's find out" and is prepared to be surprised. She has never had a patient exactly like this one before.

The therapist asks questions which stimulate associations and leads patients to explore what they could not do alone. They are encouraged to hold onto painful and contradictory evidence, to experience conflict, and to suspend judgment until they have all the facts. There is always implicit support in the sessions, but at times patients may need more: they need explicit support, reassurance and advice. In time, with experience, the therapist develops a feeling for a balance between how much support is needed and how much to let the patient struggle without intervening.

In thinking about the role of the therapist, it is helpful to remember that Harry Stack Sullivan described the role as a "participant observer." The therapist observes:

1. What is going on in the patient.
2. What is going on between the patient and the environment.
3. What is going in the therapist.

COURSE OF THERAPY

The patient, with the help of the therapist, is facing not only his symptoms, but also his triumphs and failures, fears, guilt, fantasies, shame, ambitions, hopes and yearnings. In collaboration with the therapist, he is painting the most accurate and complete picture of himself that he ever dared look at.

The therapist observes what the patient says and how he says it. He listens to the words but also observes the body language. Is this a superficial reporting of events or expressed with appropriate affect? If the former, the therapist asks about accompanying feelings and what followed his actions. This may help the patient to begin to seriously think about his behavior.

We also want the patient to explain what his words mean, especially psychological terms that he may not have really understood.

Clinical Illustrations:

1. Patient: "I think I must be manic-depressive."
Therapist: "Why do you say that?"
Patient: "Some days I'm so happy and then suddenly for no reason, I'm sad and don't care about anything. I can't figure it out."
Therapist: "You mean you are puzzled by mood swings?"
Patient: "Yeah, I guess that's what I mean."

2. Patient: "Some days I think I'm going crazy."
Therapist: "Tell me about 'crazy'?"
Patient: "I can't think straight, can't make decisions. Afraid I'll end up in the hospital, and never get out."
Therapist: "That's part of the depression. When the depression is better, your concentration improves and your thinking becomes what it used to be."

Dealing with Problems

Patients may, or may not, be aware of their problems. The first step obviously is to help them recognize that one exists and to stop denying or rationalizing. Alcoholics typically have difficulty recognizing the true state of affairs. They like to think they are "social drinkers," drink only before dinner and at parties. It may take much discussion of the extent, ramification and consequences of his drinking before a realistic picture appears. The therapist may be the first to see this clearly, and then she helps the patient see it. Also, overprotective parents have difficulty in recognizing that, at times, they hate their children and what they call discipline is really hostility and punitive behavior.

Other patients recognize their problems but may insist on unrealistic solutions: the woman who detests her husband but will not get a divorce because of religious beliefs. She continues to insist that her husband change although he has demonstrated over time that he cannot or will not. The patient finally faced the painful reality that she would either have to live with him, as he is, or get a divorce. She will have to resolve the dilemma herself.

Some patients greatly magnify problems and may panic. They feel helpless and see the situation as hopeless. If guilt, rage and depression can be minimized, the problems may be defined more clearly and their consequences estimated realistically. There are always optimal ways of dealing even with very bad situations. They are "less bad" than the alternatives.

Good therapists help the patient salvage what he can from the wreckage. Neurotics tend to make bad situations worse; if they can't have exactly what they want, then "to hell with it all." Therapists try to temper these self-destructive impulses, help the patient see the problem realistically and make effective use of his resources.

Clinical Illustration:

This was a 40-year-old stockbroker and investor who had recently lost $800,000 in the market. "Just two phone calls and I lost all that money." He was bitter, profoundly depressed, felt hopeless, thought of suicide. From the history I learned that he was the "black sheep" of the family, had dropped out of college and was the only sibling who was neither a doctor or lawyer. He wanted to be a professional baseball player but couldn't make it to the big leagues. After several attempts at various careers, he became a stockbroker. Here, he did extremely well, until with two bad trades he lost all that money, became depressed and sought therapy.

The first few sessions were filled with expressions of guilt and despair, thoughts of suicide. After the intensity of his anguish diminished, we began to explore the extent and consequences of the financial disaster.

Therapist: "Will you have to sell your home?"
Patient: "No, I paid off the mortgage when I was rich. I listened to my wife that time. Lucky."
Therapist: "Will you have to take the children out of private school?"
Patient: "No, I can manage that. After I pay all the debts, I still have enough for that."
Therapist: "Then what will you have to give up?"
Patient: "Well, I'll have to work harder. No winter vacation this year, we will do less entertaining, keep my old car for a few more years, etc."
Therapist: "It seems like your family will survive; the biggest blow was to your pride."

By defining the consequences, the problem became manageable. Follow up: the patient continued in the market and in time was again quite successful. He apparently learned from the experience and was more cautious. He also listened to his wife more.

Another important decision for the therapist is when to let the patient struggle with the problem himself and when to help him. Mistakes are made in both directions. Sometimes the patient is struggling with a problem that is far beyond his capabilities. This is no time for analysis; he needs direct advice and perhaps intervention by friends and relatives. Mistakes are also made when an overly zealous therapist tries to struggle with problems which were better left to the patient. This may result in an awkward and troublesome situation for the therapist. Therapists need to respect their own limitations. With experience, therapists make fewer mistakes.

The Disillusioning Process

In the course of therapy, we can distinguish another ongoing process which we may call a "disillusioning process." The patient is learning that he isn't the person he thinks he is, or that he "should" be. He begins to see his inconsistencies, contradictions and ambivalences. Some of the traits of which he was so proud are really not all that wonderful. He has his full share of human frailties. The reverse side of the coin is that he is also not that bad. He may not be so wonderful, but he is also not that terrible. The result of this disillusioning process is that he begins to have a more realistic picture of his actual self, who he really is.

Paradoxical Therapeutic Reaction

This happens frequently: the patient is getting better, but feels worse. She is making good progress, gaining insight, making constructive changes in her life but feels uneasy, more anxious. This is called a paradoxical therapeutic reaction. The reason for it is that change is difficult. The bad old ways were familiar, she knew what to expect. Change also involves changes in one's self-concept:

"Is this really me? I am doing these things that I never did before. Can I keep it up?"

The woman who finally leaves an abusive husband faces problems that she never faced before: a new life-style, financial worries, criticism from some relatives, etc. Leaving her husband solved a problem that appeared hopeless. Now, she is facing realistic problems with a much better chance of coping well. In time, the patient appreciates the change and wonders why she didn't do it sooner.

Support and Reassurance

As previously mentioned, there are times when the patient's anxiety and distress are so great that he needs quick relief. There is support in the opportunity to ventilate and especially in the helpful relationship with a therapist who is also concerned with the patient's problems. However, more explicit help may be needed. This is a time to stop discussion of topics which disturb the patient; insight can wait. This is not the time to point out his inconsistencies, exaggerations or rationalizations.

The patient may be helped by advice: pointing out resources that are available to him, as well as people or situations to avoid at this time. The therapist may be able to help with information that is useful to the patient. Therapy is also a learning experience: almost always patients learn from their therapist, and the reverse is true as well.

Reassurance is usually of only transient benefit; it is superficial since it does not deal with the unconscious determinants of the symptom. It does not address the meaning the symptom has for the patient, and why he can't let go. These will be resolved only much later in the course of therapy and will then provide basic, long-term resolution. However, when the patient is acutely distressed and struggling ineffectively, reassurance is indicated. The patient needs a respite, and long-term goals can wait.

When the therapist uses such cliches as: "There's nothing to worry about" or "We'll cross that bridge when we get to it," he is not being logical, nor completely honest. He is using the authority vested in him by the patient, to stop her thinking for herself and to trust him. It covers up problems; they will have to be uncovered and dealt with at a later time. Reassurance should be used sparingly. It should not be used because the therapist becomes too anxious and frightened by the patient's symptoms. Of course, effective medications are now available which relieve suffering. They have a very definite place in treatment, but before prescribing them, it is necessary to find out how the patient feels about taking medication. The therapist should also be clear about his objectives in using them and what other complications medication brings into the therapist-patient relationship.

Clinical Illustration

The patient was a young woman who just had a bitter argument with her mother-in-law. She kept berating herself for not handling it more diplomatically. She knew her husband would be upset when he heard about it. After a considerable period of self-flagellation, the therapist intervened with: "Well, what can you expect from a mother-in-law?" The patient was relieved. The intrapsychic conflict was shifted to an interpersonal one, and the conventional wisdom that in our society, mothers-in law are difficult for everyone. Later on, at a more appropriate time, they would discuss the patient's feelings for her mother-in-law and how these contributed to a stormy relationship.

Personal Questions

At times, patients ask personal questions of the therapist: "Are you married?" "Whom did you vote for in the last election? "Do you have children?"

In ordinary encounters, when someone asks a question, we respond with an answer. The answer may be candid or evasive, but it would be rude not to answer. However, the relationship between patient and therapist is unique. It is wise to consider before revealing something about yourself. What is behind the question? Is it just friendly interest or does the patient have some problem with it? A good general rule is that behind every question may be a problem. Here, it may be wiser to answer a question with a question. Therapists need to exercise caution about revealing information about themselves.

Many things about the therapist are quickly apparent: his name, age, how he dresses, how he speaks. Diplomas indicate where he trained. The office furnishings also reflect something about the person. However, we don't want personal characteristics of the therapist to be intrusive and interfere with the therapy. We also want to encourage the patient to fantasize about the therapist. For these reasons, we want to keep the therapist largely an unknown to the patient. It also gives us a good opportunity to learn more about the patient. The same considerations apply if the patient invites you to a Christmas party or similar social event. It is wisest to decline, but like most rules, there are times when exceptions may be made.

Of course, there are occasions when you may answer personal questions with beneficial effects on the course of therapy. If the patient is facing some crisis which the therapist has previously lived through, it may be appropriate to reveal it. It demonstrates to the patient that the therapist is a human being, subject to all the ills that people are heir to and able to be empathic with the troubles of the patient.

Clinical Example:

Soon after the initial interview started, an African-American woman asked how I felt about blacks and would I be uncomfortable having one for a patient. I said: "I'll answer your question, but first I would like to ask how you feel about white people." She answered that she had encountered quite a bit of prejudice and was generally wary in dealing with whites. However, since she always sought competent help, in addition to a black internist, she now had a white dentist and a white accountant whom she trusted completely. I then answered that while I had treated few African-Americans, she would be just another patient. In the exchange, I learned something about the patient, and she did about me.

Silent Periods

While we want to use the available time efficiently, periods of silence may be valuable also. If the patient is comfortable with the silence, and it is not too long, just wait. If the silence becomes lengthy, the therapist may bring up a topic which needs further elaboration. Always ask how the patient feels about the silence. Did the patient expect that she would never waste a single minute of every session? At some time it would be appropriate to point out that this is unrealistic. If the patient complains that "she feels like a bump on a log," she can be reassured that these periods do occur and that when she can talk, she will. *It is a mistake to cut down the length of the sessions, or the frequency, because the patient runs out of things to say.* This makes everything worse. Everyone has a lot to say, if not blocked.

Periods of silence may be valuable if the patient gets in better touch with feelings, old memories, or fantasies. Of course, long periods of silence frequently represent resistance, especially transference reactions. These need to be analyzed. Another possibility needs to be considered—long periods of silence may result from severe depressions which may require medication, or in some instances, hospitalization.

Dealing with Resistance

A classic definition of psychoanalysis is that it is the treatment of resistance and transference. Attention to resistance is as important as the development of insight. Therapists need to be alert to the many forms resistance may take and deal with it adequately.

Clinical Illustration

The patient phoned the clinic and cancelled the upcoming session. He kept the next session but did not mention anything about the missed session. Toward the end of the session, the therapist said: "You didn't say anything about missing the previous meeting." The patient was taken aback, ill at ease and had nothing to say for several minutes and then began to discuss his pattern of avoiding certain situations. This confrontation dealt with the patient's pattern of avoiding unpleasant or awkward situations which the patient does on many occasions. This behavior interferes with therapy. The therapist did not ask: "Why did you miss the last session?" The patient could have answered with a variety of excuses, most probably rationalizations. However, *the therapist asked about his avoidance.* This opens up for discussion one of his major defenses: how he uses it in all other areas of his life and what it does for him, and to him.

Patients give many reasons for coming late, missing sessions, or terminating therapy. The reasons are financial, pressure of time, problems with children, etc., etc. Sometimes they are valid, many times they are not. They often are rationalizations in the service of resistance.

Patients bring up many "realistic" reasons why they cannot continue therapy, or even consider it. Many who complain about cost can afford expensive clothes, cars, vacations, etc. Those who plead the pressure of time, often have enough time for a great variety of social and athletic activities. There are realistic barriers, of course, but many times it is a question of priorities.

Patients who are well-motivated and committed to therapy present an interesting picture: they rarely are late or miss sessions, they always find another baby-sitter if the regular one gets sick, if the car conks out, they borrow the neighbor's, and so on. Their behavior tells you how they feel about therapy: that it is one of the of the most important things they ever attempted.

Periodic Review

It is useful to review the progress of therapy at periodic intervals: what was done and what was accomplished. Instead of considering only individual sessions, it is helpful to review a period of the last 4 to 6 sessions. Looking at this segment of time, it is easier to determine progress, or the lack of it.

It is not enough to have the general feeling that the patient is getting better, we want to know the particulars of how he is better. Does he speak more freely, in better contact with his feelings, has given up some illusions and rationalizations, gained a better picture of his actual self, have better insight into his actions and feelings? Are the symptoms relieved to some extent? Is there a good working alliance, have some negative transference reactions been resolved?

In addition to reviewing a period of several sessions, there are times when it is helpful to review the previous session. With patients who are quick to agree with interpretations but don't seem to apply the insights in their daily lives and with those who have difficulty maintaining continuity in treatment, it may be very useful to review the previous session. "Before we go on to new material, what did we talk about at the last session?" This confrontation may be very stressful and should be used with discrimination.

SUMMING UP

Each therapist develops a personal style of conducting therapy. Some of the recommendations given above are to be used as guidelines. There are valid exceptions to all rules. Therapists conduct the therapy according to the needs of the patient and using the resources of the patient. Therapists have the greater responsibility, they are responsible for everything the patient says, or leaves unsaid. However, they are not obligated to "cure" every patient, only to do their professional best.

RECOMMENDED READING

1. Basch, M.F.: *Practicing Psychotherapy: A Case Book.* New York, Basic Books, 1992.
2. Gabbard, G.O.: *Psychodynamic Psychiatry in Clinical Practice. The DSM-IV Edition.* Washington D.C., American Psychiatric Press, 1994.
3. Greenberg, J.R., & Mitchell, S.A.: *Object Relations in Psychoanalytic Theory.* Cambridge, MA, Harvard, 1983.
4. Greenberg, S.I.: Analysis once a week. *American Journal Psychoanalysis* 46:327-335, 1986.
5. Ingram, D.H.: Reassurance in analytic therapy. *American Journal Psychoanalysis* 57: 221-241, 1997.
6. Wallerstein, R.S.: *The Talking Cures-The Psychoanalyses and the Psychotherapies.* New Haven, CT, Yale University Press, 1996.

Chapter 9

ANXIETY AND DEPRESSION

Anxiety and depression are such important issues for therapists that they deserve additional attention. Also, understanding the dynamics are of great practical help. Beginning with the DSM-III, anxiety was classified as a disorder rather than a symptom of unconscious conflict that is present in many psychiatric disorders. The division into general anxiety disorder, phobias, panic and obsessive-compulsive disorders is arbitrary, and many patients do not fit neatly into these categories.

For the dynamic therapist treating any patient where anxiety is a prominent feature of the clinical picture, the concept of *signal anxiety* is helpful. This holds that anxiety results when there is a threat that unacceptable thoughts and feelings may come into awareness because the defenses are no longer adequate to keep them repressed. Anxiety is a signal of danger and mobilizes the defenses to keep the conflict from becoming conscious. Therapy, therefore, involves a collaboration between patient and therapist to explore the developmental origins of the anxiety.

Depression also holds a unique role in the history of analysis and psychotherapy. The term is used for a mood, a symptom or a disorder. It may be the most common problem which therapists encounter. In addition to the major categories such as dysthymia, major depression, and bipolar disorder, it may also appear as a symptom in almost any psychiatric entity. The classic concept of the dynamics was that it resulted from anger turned inward, against the self, on the loss of an emotionally significant object. The self was identified with the lost object. Guilt and loss of self-esteem regularly accompanied the process. Depression differed from grief in that, in the latter, the loss was of a realistically significant figure and self-esteem was not impaired. Later contributions to the theory emphasized the discrepancy between ideals and reality ("I'm not good enough") and failed interpersonal relationships in childhood.

TREATMENT OF ANXIETY

Like one, that on a lonesome road
Doth walk in fear and dread,
And having once turned round, walks on
And turns no more his head:
Because he knows, a frightful fiend
Doth close behind him tread.

Coleridge, *The Rime of the Ancient Mariner*

Poets have the gift to present fundamental truths about human beings in a few, short lines. Here, the poet illustrates a basic problem in anxiety: that the person is afraid to face and examine carefully what he is afraid of. He really does not know what the danger is, but erroneously assumes that it is too much for him to cope with and keeps on running.

In treating a patient with anxiety, the therapist needs to explore:

1.What is the danger?
2.Why is the patient vulnerable?
3.Why is the patient unable to deal with it?

The following brief case report may illustrate some of these issues.

Case Report of a Phobia

The patient was a 47-year-old man recently separated from his wife and going through a stormy divorce. At the initial interview, he was tense, agitated and constantly worrying about the effects of the divorce on his two sons, who were both in high school. He had been married over twenty years and felt that they had been a happy family when the children were young. The wife was a devoted, if overprotective mother. He taught at a large university, made good progress up the academic ladder and was now a full professor, with tenure. The wife made most of the decisions, which was fine with the patient, except on those infrequent occasions when she drank too much or ran up large debts. It was hard for him to confront her on these occasions. In the past five years, the wife's drinking became much worse; she was verbally and physically abusive at home and even in public. She was treated by several psychiatrists with no benefit.

In the course of our sessions, I learned that the patient was an only child, whose father was killed in an auto accident when he was two and whose step-father was distant and stern. He was an excellent student, but he would have preferred being taller and a better athlete. I also learned that public speaking was a torture for him. He had no trouble lecturing to students, but presenting a paper at a national meeting was something else. If he could not avoid it, he would fortify himself with a small amount of propanalol and painfully stammer his way through it.

Therapist: "Tell me about public speaking."
Patient: "If it's a large audience, it's torture. My name is called, and all those eyes are looking at me and I force myself to get up and stand on the platform and pray that I'll get through."
Therapist: "What can go wrong?"
Patient: "I'll stammer, mispronounce words, lose my train of thought and make a spectacle of myself. I'll do something stupid and everyone will laugh. I think: 'what I doing up here?' Here I am talking to all these experts.'"
Therapist: "But aren't you also an expert?"
Patient: "You're right. But I have to keep on reminding myself that that's so."

Comment: In time, the patient could speak in public with relative comfort. He began to accept that he was an expert in his field, that he had something worthwhile to say, and that it didn't have to be a perfect presentation.

The patient did well with insight-oriented therapy. He was intelligent, verbal and prepared to be helped by psychotherapy. He required some support only in the early sessions; after that I could sit back and listen as he analyzed the problems and made good, although painful, decisions. I enjoyed working with him. He made good progress with his major difficulties: inability to assert himself and poor self-esteem. He began to feel like the middle-aged, competent man he really was.

Although it hardly does justice to the complexities of his character and difficulties in living, for insurance purposes my diagnosis was:

Axis I: Generalized Anxiety Disorder, and
Axis II: Dependent Personality Disorder.

TREATMENT OF DEPRESSION

The dynamics of depression help us formulate a plan of psychotherapy for the patient, but the total clinical picture requires some difficult decisions. Is the patient so depressed that he requires medication as well as psychotherapy? In which case, how does the patient feel about medication? Is the patient suicidal? This requires exploring the home situation and determining who provides support for this patient. Hospitalization may also need to be considered. No uncovering psychotherapy can begin until these issues are resolved.

When the patient is ready for psychotherapy, the issues of guilt, relationships, ambivalences, self-worth, hopelessness and the expression of anger need to be explored. Probing should be done carefully, as these can be explosive issues. The therapist who leans to the analytic model approaches the patient with an attitude of "let's find out," exploring for meanings and origins without prejudgment as to their relative importance. They are active but try to let the patient formulate the questions to which she wants answers. Depending on the degree of depression, these patients may have difficulty in speaking, and long, unproductive silences will result. This is the time for the therapist to ask carefully phrased questions to help the patient talk. This is not the time for free-association.

Case Illustration

Dr. H., in his early thirties, was an associate professor at one of the colleges in the area. He was referred because he had been depressed since his wife left him two months ago and rebuffed all his attempts at reconciliation. The following highlights of his life story came out in the course of the early sessions.

He was born and raised in an affluent suburb of a large Midwestern city. The father was a successful salesman who travelled a great deal and away from home much of the time. When home, he enlivened an otherwise bleak atmosphere. The mother usually showed little emotion but on occasion would display great anger and could be very cruel. One of his earliest memories, from the age of four, was refusing to do something his mother told him to. Thereupon, she said she didn't want him for a son, put on his hat and coat and pushed him out the door. Only much later did she let him back in. The parents argued frequently and bitterly. They divorced when he was fifteen.

As was customary in their community, he was given music lessons, attended religious school and was sent to sleep-away camp in the summer. He was a good athlete and thoroughly enjoyed camp. It was here that he met the girl he later married. He was an excellent student in high school, college and graduate school. Upon graduation, he worked in research and development for a large firm and then accepted an appointment at the college.

He married at 25, his wife was 4 years younger. She was pretty and very popular ("everybody liked her"). They argued frequently. He complained that she was lazy, spent too much money and was not intellectual enough. She complained that he did not spend enough time with her, was stingy and did not care for anything except work. The patient admitted that he was a "workaholic" and that when he was busy, he barely spoke to her. He did not take his wife's complaints seriously and was stunned when she walked out. His depression became deeper when she refused all overtures at reconciliation.

In the early sessions, he would start with: "What shall I talk about?". The basic rule ("Say everything that comes to mind") was of no help. After a minute or two of silence, I would ask questions ("How do you feel?" "What kind of week was it?", etc.) usually about his work, colleagues, wife, mother, and so on. This went on for over a year before he could speak with some spontaneity and "free-association."

The breakup of his marriage was the first area we worked through. He realized that it was not a good relationship and that he had not been happy. They both contributed to the difficulties. He had not treated her as an equal partner. He felt he deserved more because he worked harder and he had suffered more. He needed her but was afraid of closeness, afraid of being exploited or rejected. His need for approval was very great—from friends, colleagues, students and others.

Feelings that had been suppressed and repressed came to the surface. In time, he could talk about the great loneliness and despair he felt as a child. He was envious of neighbors who lived differently ("they were a normal family"). It was safer not to want things. He became aware of anger at his father for abandoning him to his "crazy" mother. The great difficulties with his mother were partly resolved. In time, he could recognize that she was an unhappy and disturbed woman, but the bitterness and anger remained. He recognized that he could not solve all his problems by intellect alone.

In his relationship to me, he was cautious and distant in the beginning. Intellectually, he "knew" he could trust me but was too defensive to really open up. Early in the course of treatment, he was critical of analysis in general and of the Clinic and me in particular, but never got very angry. We discussed all the issues. Toward the end of the treatment, I was a trusted collaborator whom he liked and respected.

What happened to H. during the nearly four years he was in treatment? He decided that there was more to life than work and made efforts to achieve a better balance in his personal life. He recognized that while he would like a national reputation, he was not willing to do all the work that would be required. People were more important. He bought a sports car and new furniture for the apartment, developed a circle of friends, organized a musical group and entertained more. With women, his pattern changed from an adolescent style of dating with much anxiety, fear of rejection and overemphasis on sex, to more mature and relaxed relationships. He was a more effective teacher, more concerned with students' problems than with his image. He became closer to his father, but the relationship with his mother was still painful. He felt that it would never be good.

The patient moved to another city when he accepted an appointment at a large university. Two years later, I heard from a psychiatrist in this other city that the patient had suffered a recurrent depression. This time, he accepted medication and responded well to the prescribed antidepressants.

Comments: The recurrence notwithstanding, the patient and I both felt that he had benefitted a great from psychotherapy. The optimal regime would have included medication from the very beginning, but the patient refused it then. It would have probably shortened the course of treatment. Also, the patient was seen once a week. It would have been better to see him more frequently at the beginning, but his schedule, and mine, did not permit it.

RECOMMENDED READING

1. Gaylin, W. (Ed.): *The Meaning of Despair.* New York, Science House, 1968.
2. Klerman, G.L., Weissman, M., Rounsaville, B.J., & Chevron, E.S.: *Interpersonal Psychotherapy of Depression.* New York, Basic Books, 1984.
3. Yalom, I.D.: *Existential Psychotherapy.* New York, Basic Books, 1980.

Chapter 10

TERMINATION

There are two frequent problems in ending therapy: the patient wants to end too soon and the therapist has difficulty letting go.

The tendency of many patients is to want to stop too soon. As soon as they begin to feel better, they are quick to declare that therapy was successful and are ready to stop. Many elements enter into the decision. First, there is the formidable cost of treatment, especially when they no longer have insurance coverage. Then the time and effort involved in keeping appointments is considerable. Also, patients are uneasy about what may turn up if they keep on probing. And then there are patients who feel that treatment can go on forever unless they call a halt.

When patients bring up the subject of termination, I often say that this decision is as important as that of starting. The decision should be made carefully and deliberately after adequate discussion. This is a good time to refer to the notes of the initial interviews and review what the patient's objectives were at that time. We can then discuss what has been done so far and what changes have resulted. The patient may have made good progress but realize that more remains to be done. We should encourage this incentive for further personal growth. We should try to avoid giving the impression that treatment is interminable. Treatment may end when both patient and therapist agree that they have substantially achieved their objectives. This does not mean that the patient cannot return sometime in the future to discuss some new development in his life. There is a parallel with formal education: learning never ends, but we do get a diploma from college after all the appropriate course work has been done.

If the subject of termination comes up close to the summer, I may suggest that the patient stop for July and August and return for a visit in September and we can then discuss how well the patient fared. If this discussion occurs in the fall, I suggest stopping from Thanksgiving until after the New Year. Of course, with many patients there is no chance for discussion, they just phone in, and cancel their next appointment.

70

Therapists also have difficulties with termination. Many are reluctant to see patients leave before they are on a firm footing. They feel that all the good work that was accomplished with so much effort may be placed in jeopardy by too early termination. Some therapists have difficulty with termination because they have become dependent on the patient; the relationship meets some unrecognized need of theirs. They may believe that the patient needs them; no other therapist can do as much for them. This calls for serious self-analysis.

When the issue of termination comes up, the therapist who has been reviewing the progress at intervals, now will try to consolidate the gains. It is helpful to look back and see how far the patient has come. What has been accomplished? Are the symptoms better? Does the patient have a better sense of self, use his talents more effectively, better relationships, more realistic goals?

And then there are patients who have trouble letting go. Some regression and dependency occurs frequently in therapy, but at the appropriate time, these traits are analyzed with the objective of helping the patient to become more independent and self-sufficient. It is poor therapy to continue when this serves mainly to prolong the patient's neurotic dependency needs.

And yet, when all that has been said, there are some patients who are not entirely adequate to face the many challenges of our competitive society. They need a rudder to help them navigate, and a meeting several times a year with the therapist may be of enormous benefit. This, again, is another difficult decision for the therapist.

PART 2
SPECIAL SITUATIONS

Chapter 11

SUICIDAL PATIENTS

Patients who threaten suicide, or make attempts, are a source of "endless disquiet." In dealing with such patients the therapist needs to be as careful and as thorough as he or she possibly can. The case notes should be clear and comprehensive. Never erase anything; write additional notes if needed to clarify some point but do not erase. Few events in the life of a therapist will be more traumatic than the suicide of a patient. It is the ultimate narcissistic injury. The therapist will be blamed, and often sued, even if he or she has done everything possible to prevent it. The therapist makes a convenient target for the projection of guilt by family members. The general public's perception is that suicide is preventable; whenever a suicide occurs, they look for someone to blame. This myth is widespread in spite of the fact that the incidence of suicide has not decreased significantly in the last 30 years.

BASIC SUICIDOLOGY

A simple definition of suicide is the intentional taking of one's own life. A more useful, if cumbersome, definition is that by E.S. Shneidman: "a conscious act of self-induced annihilation, best understood as a multidimensional malaise in a needful individual who defines an issue for which suicide is perceived as the best solution" (The Definition of Suicide: An Essay. New York, John Wiley & Sons, 1985).

There are more than 30,000 deaths by suicide each year in the United States. It is the eighth leading cause of death with an incidence of approximately 12 per 100,000 per year. The incidence has not changed significantly in the last 30 years. The ratio of men to women is 3:1, although women attempt it more frequently. The ratio of whites to nonwhites is 2:1. Two thirds of all suicides are white men. The highest rate is in elderly white men living alone.

More than 90 percent of suicidal individuals have a diagnosable mental disorder. Two-thirds of all suicides are associated with depression and alcoholism. Fifteen percent of schizophrenics die by suicide. Almost all studies also indicate that a small number, two to six percent, are not mentally ill. Of course, many who are diagnosed with a mental disorder are in good contact with reality and competent.

Accurate data on attempts is more difficult to obtain than on completed suicides since many attempts are not reported. Also, there is no consistency in terminology and in distinguishing gestures from attempts. Attempters are a different, and much larger population, than completed ("successful") suicides. They are younger; the peak rate is in the 20-24 age group. Females predominate and overdose/poisoning rather than firearms is the most common method. Although these are distinct populations, there is some overlapping between them. Those who make an attempt with an active method, leave notes and make minimal provision for rescue constitute a high risk group; six percent of them will commit suicide in the following year. (Tuckman & Youngman, Journal of Clinical Psychology 24:17-19, 1968).

DYNAMICS

Why do people kill themselves? It is an intensely personal decision and obviously the subject is no longer alive to tell us what was on his mind immediately before the event. However, we do have a wealth of information from the life-histories of suicides and those who have fortuitously survived serious attempts. Most suicides are "escape suicides," they can no longer face the pain, emptiness and hopelessness. They feel that all they have valued is gone, life has become meaningless.

Another major category is the aggressive or vindictive type. They are angry at the world and will get back at those who have treated them unfairly. The great anger and rage which he cannot express is turned inward against the self. Karl Menninger called it "murder in the 180 degree." There are also individuals who live recklessly; they take risks which add zest to their lives or gain them attention and admiration. In these individuals, it is difficult to separate accidental deaths from suicide.

There are also instances where suicide may be called altruistic or self-sacrificing. They end their lives so they will no longer be a burden or that others may benefit in some way. One other category of suicide needs to be discussed: "rational suicide." This is a controversial issue and many experienced clinicians feel that suicide is never rational: when a person asks for aid-in-dying, he or she is mentally ill. Others disagree and feel that in some circumstances suicide may be the rational choice of a competent individual. They agree with the philosopher Bonhoeffer who wrote: "Sometimes suicide is a man's attempt to give a final human meaning to a life which has become humanly meaningless."

PREDICTION AND PREVENTION

The great majority of individuals who eventually kill themselves do give indication of their intent. However, suicide thoughts, threats and attempts are difficult to interpret. From demographic and clinical data, we can recognize that certain individuals belong in a high risk group, but the identification of the particular person who will kill himself is not feasible. Existing suicide intent scales are of little value in prediction as they lack sensitivity and specificity. The Beck Hopelessness Scale is one of the best but is still more useful in research than in practice. In current practice, the ability to predict suicide is severely limited.

The ability to prevent suicide also is limited; many feel that often we postpone, rather than prevent, suicide. Still, there are indicators which alert therapists that the danger is great. In vulnerable individuals, certain events frequently precipitate attempts and completed suicides. These involve loss of some kind: death of a friend or relative, divorce, financial reverses, loss of a job or business, lawsuits, and so on. Sometimes rather trivial events may be precipitants.

Jan Fawcett and co-workers have written extensively about risk factors and predictors of suicide (American Journal Psychiatry, 147: 1189-1194, 1990). They emphasize that intense anxiety, panic attacks, insomnia, anger, depression, and alcohol abuse are indicators of high risk for the shortterm (i.e. within 6 months). Hopelessness and previous attempts are indicators of long-term risk (i.e., 1-10 years).

TREATMENT/MANAGEMENT

The treatment of these difficult patients is made more difficult by countertransference. Therapists regularly are intimidated by them or become hostile when they feel the patients are manipulative and are exploiting them. If the therapist feels that he has the total responsibility for keeping the patient alive, he is functioning under a crushing burden. It is also an impossible task. The therapist can only make a careful examination, identify the mental disorder that is usually present and initiate appropriate treatment. That is all that is possible.

In most cases, medication will be indicated: antidepressants, tranquillizers and neuroleptics. If there is alcohol abuse or dependence in the clinical picture, referral to an appropriate program may be necessary. The most difficult decision is whether to hospitalize the patient or not. If the patient will consent to it, the hospital may be the best place to start treatment. Hospitalization does provide the greatest safety over the short term but has many drawbacks. It is the most restrictive mode of treatment and still carries, for many, a stigma.

If involuntary commitment is decided on, the hospital staff is cast in an adversarial role and interferes with the long-term goal of helping the patient take charge of his own life. Patients can't stay in the hospital forever. And, of course, suicides do occur in the hospital, and they are at greater risk in the first two weeks after discharge. Still, the most appropriate place for a suicidal patient in imminent danger is an inpatient psychiatric unit. These are difficult decisions.

PRACTICAL SUGGESTIONS

With all new patients, as part of the life history the patient should be asked about suicide thoughts and attempts. All threats are to be taken seriously but not literally. If you feel that the patient is at significant risk, you need to get as much information as you can, and quickly. It is wise to do a mental status examination and consider psychologic testing and/or consultation. It is also wise to inform a responsible relative or friend. This breach of confidentiality is unfortunate but necessary. If you are very uncomfortable with the patient, refer him or her. You don't have to treat every patient referred to you. No therapist should have several suicidal patients at one time.

Appropriate psychotherapy is always indicated. In the emergent stage, the patient needs support from the therapist and from all resources available in the family and community, opportunity to ventilate, etc. For the chronic suicidal individuals, the therapist has the most difficult task of helping the patient achieve a life that is meaningful.

When I sense that there is a power struggle with the patient, I sometimes say: "If you are really determined to kill yourself, one day you will. But since you can only do it once, you had better be sure that you pick the right time." When I think confrontation may help, I have said to a young, married woman: "Do you think your husband will marry again?" Or I may say: "Who will be the mourners at your funeral?" The important thing about such interventions is appropriate timing. The therapist who is frightened by the patient tends to reassure too much and promise too much. The therapist who is angry at the patient tends to minimize that the patient is suffering and in despair. The following table of risk factors may be helpful:

Table 1.

```
┌─────────────────────────────────────────────────────────┐
│              RISK FACTORS FOR COMPLETED SUICIDE           │
│                                                           │
│  Demographic                                              │
│          Male, elderly                                    │
│          White                                            │
│          Divorced, widowed, single                        │
│          No children under 18, or pets, at home           │
│                                                           │
│  Clinical                                                 │
│          Family History                                   │
│                  Relatives with major depression          │
│                  Suicide in relatives                     │
│          Past Personal History                            │
│                  Episodes of depression                   │
│                  Previous suicide attempts                │
│          Diagnosis                                        │
│                  Major depression, Bipolar Disorder       │
│                  Alcohol abuse /dependence                │
│                  Schizophrenia                            │
│                  Other Psychiatric Disorders              │
│          Symptoms                                         │
│                  Anxiety (severe), Panic Attacks          │
│                  Suicide ideation                         │
│                  Hopelessness                             │
│                                                           │
│  Precipitating Events                                     │
│          Disruption of significant relationship           │
│          Loss of employment /business                     │
│          Disgrace /humiliation                            │
│          Legal problems /arrest /jail                     │
│          Recent discharge from psychiatric hospital       │
│          Loss of therapist                                │
└─────────────────────────────────────────────────────────┘
```

Chapter 12

COMBINING MEDICATION AND PSYCHOTHERAPY

When patients are receiving medication along with therapy, we may have complications. We now need to consider how the therapist feels about medication, how the patient feels about medication, and what the patient thinks, the therapist thinks, about the medication. Why was it prescribed? The situation becomes even more complicated when we have two therapists, one for psychotherapy and the other who prescribes and supervises the medication. Instead of a relatively simple twosome, we now have a very complex threesome.

There are now many effective pharmacologic agents in widespread use. Psychotherapists can expect that some patients who are referred to them are already on one medication or another. Or, in the course of psychotherapy, clinical conditions may change and it becomes clear that medication is also indicated. In the current climate, therapists cannot expect to avoid the complications that medications contribute to the conduct of psychotherapy.

We cannot discuss all aspects of this issue in great detail, but we can alert the therapist to some of the important considerations when we combine medication with psychotherapy. Medication makes therapy possible for many patients by moderating severe anxiety or depression, but it adds a host of complications. With a new patient, my preference is to start with psychotherapy alone, unless medication is absolutely indicated. I have been pleasantly surprised at how often the support provided by the working alliance relieves anxiety sufficiently and permits psychotherapy to move along at a good pace. Of course, I have no hesitation in adding medication where it is definitely indicated.

THE PATIENT

How does the patient feel about medication? Many are uneasy with any medication; they try to avoid all "drugs." They prefer herbs and "natural" products. They worry about side-effects and possible addiction. Others are frightened by medication because this means he is a "real patient" with a serious disorder. They can accept psychotherapy because that is like talking to a confidant or seeking advice and counsel.

Some welcome medication because that fits in with their idea that they have an inherited medical condition, a "chemical imbalance." They are innocent victims and therefore not responsible for problems that have developed.

The patient's attitude toward medication is dependent to a large extent on the relationship with the therapist. With a good working alliance or positive transference, medication is seen in a positive light. The therapist is giving him extra attention; they are prepared to believe that the pills are special and will be very effective. The mere presence of the bottle with the doctor's name in the medicine cabinet is reassuring. It functions as a transitional object (e.g. a baby's blanket).

On the other hand, when there is a negative transference, medication may be seen as a sign that the doctor doesn't care about him and is taking the least burdensome way of treating him. Needless to say, this attitude does not help the effectiveness of the medication.

When medication is prescribed in addition to psychotherapy, there may be some question in the patient's mind as to which modality is helping. Why are both necessary? Is the "talking cure" helping, or is it largely a waste of time and money? Another complication is that manipulative patients may spend so much time talking about the medication that they divert attention from more significant, and uncomfortable, issues.

THE THERAPIST

Therapists need to be clear why they are prescribing, or recommending, medication. Is it definitely indicated? Does the severity of the anxiety or depression interfere with the psychotherapy? Will combined therapy be more effective? Will medication make psychotherapy unnecessary?

Or is the therapist afraid of the patient's potential for violence and trying for better control by chemical means? Does the therapist doubt the value of psychotherapy? One of the benefits of therapy for therapists is that they have firsthand experience of its value.

Sometimes a patient may demand medication that he has read about in a magazine. This may lead to a power struggle between the two. The therapist may refuse to prescribe it if he feels the medication has little merit and thereby antagonize the patient. Or, he may prescribe it to placate the patient and may, or may not, resent it. Some requests of the patient may have merit, others do not. However, they are all opportunities to discuss the expectations and hopes of the patient. These discussions may be very productive.

Therapists who prescribe medication need to consider whether it will be abused or whether the patient may become addicted. If the patient is suicidal, this is another factor to take into consideration. Some psychiatrists prescribe only small amounts of medication with no refills as a safety precaution. Patients may resent the necessity for frequent refills and accuse the therapist of not trusting them. Almost always it is a mistake to be pressured into doing something that is not appropriate. Therapists can explain that they have to take responsibility for their actions. They may lose the patient or may have an opportunity to discuss why the patient insists on getting his own way, sometimes to his detriment. In the latter instance, the patient may learn something very valuable.

TWO THERAPISTS

When there are two therapists, one for psychotherapy and the other for medication, we have advantages and disadvantages. The two therapists provide more expertise and differing perspectives, which can be invaluable. The patient benefits from both. The big disadvantage is that it is harder to establish relationships with two therapists.

This arrangement facilitates intrapsychic splitting in which the patient comes to idealize one therapist and devalue the other. The danger is greatest with borderlines who tend to form unstable relationships. An excellent discussion of the problem is in an article by Waldinger and Frank (Transference and the Vicissitudes of Medication Use by Borderline Patients. *Psychiatry* 52: 416-427, 1989).

The relationship of the two therapists to each other is crucial. They need to respect each other's competence, accept their boundaries and feel free to communicate. Otherwise they may sabotage each other's efforts. Perceptive patients will detect hostilities and rivalries between them. Manipulative patients who are intent on sabotaging their treatment may present subtly different pictures to the two therapists and exacerbate the antagonisms between them. They may not be easy to find, but the efforts to find a compatible colleague are very worthwhile.

In spite of all the possible pitfalls, with most patients combined therapy with two therapists works out quite well.

Chapter 13

SEX WITH PATIENTS

and lead us not into temptation
New Testament

Throughout history we have had numerous instances of famous men ruined by sexual misadventures. In spite of their knowledge of human behavior, psychiatrists, psychologists, and other mental health workers have not always been able to resist inappropriate romantic and sexual involvement with patients. Those therapists who lead unhappy and isolated lives are vulnerable when they are exposed to close relationships with patients which may last for long periods. Patients are vulnerable because the therapeutic situation fosters regression, dependence, and trust in the authority of the therapist. Transference/ countertransference reactions distort reality for patient and therapist and lead to expectations which are impossible for fulfillment.

At various times in the past, some therapists (leaders, trainers, facilitators) of encounter and sensitivity groups tolerated or even encouraged sexual relationships. There were exotic schools of therapy which encouraged nude, mixed bathing, group therapy with all participants in the nude and other variations from the conventional. The great majority of these, if not all, have ceased to exist. All major professional organizations now explicitly condemn sexual relations with patients as unethical and destructive of therapy. The American Psychiatric Association places no time limit on the physician-patient relationship —once a patient, always a patient.

In the following discussion, for the sake of simplicity, I will describe the interactions as between a male therapist and a female patient. Of course, there are now as many women therapists as men, and sexual misconduct may also involve partners of the same sex. I am not too optimistic how much I will accomplish by this section, but since the

85

results of misconduct are often catastrophic, I feel the attempt is worthwhile. The following observations are from my own practice, from colleagues and from the literature.

The Predatory Therapist

There aren't too many psychopaths (i.e. antisocial personality disorders) among therapists, but the few there are cause a great deal of mischief. They are clever enough to avoid detection for long periods of time and often move to another town before their misdeeds catch up with them. Psychiatrists and psychologists are good judges of character and motivation in their patients, but not of their colleagues. They tend to assume that their colleagues are as honorable and ethical as they are.

The psychopathic therapist enjoys the exercise of power and the control it gives him over another person. It is not too difficult for a predatory therapist to abuse the therapeutic relationship with a trusting patient. Also, they select as victims passive-dependent patients who are not likely to complain to authorities. The most that these patients do is to stop coming. Many are ashamed or so guilt-ridden they assume that they did something wrong and tell no one.

Clinical Illustration:

This was a very attractive woman of 25, unhappily married, with many complaints: mood swings, phobias, impulsive spending sprees, etc. She had been in treatment previously with another psychiatrist, and this is a brief summary of her experience with him.

At first she was delighted with him; he was sympathetic and listened to her without interrupting. This was a pleasant change from her husband. After the first few sessions, he began calling her by her first name and sometimes held her hand. She interpreted these as indications that he liked her and was concerned. He also revealed details about his personal life including the fact that he was separated from his wife and in the process of getting a divorce.

He suggested that Vitamin B-Complex would be helpful with her excessive fatigue and that it should be started with intramuscular injections which he would do. The second injection was followed by fondling and sex. Every session now included sex. He never told her he loved her, and she could not help noting that he soon began to appear less affectionate. The final blow occurred when the patient found out that he was charging her for visits that were largely taken up with their lovemaking.

Soon after she stopped coming, the psychiatrist suddenly moved to a distant city. She later found out that the county medical society began to investigate reports of incidents similar to hers.

The Seductive Patient

There are disturbed women who devote much of their energies to sexual adventures. They are attracted to the husbands of their friends and especially consider it an accomplishment to seduce their therapist. Their motives are varied: they like the feeling that they are attractive and desirable, the feeling of power, it's an adventure and keeps them from being bored. They are ambivalent about therapy, afraid of what they may find out about themselves. In the course of therapy they may describe their sexual adventures and observe the reaction of the therapist. They also dress provocatively. Sometimes they may explicitly invite a sexual relationship ("How can you learn all about me if you won't go to bed with me?").

The appropriate course for the therapist is to explore, without delay, the patient's relationships with all the significant men in her life, past and present. Also appropriate would be to discuss how the patient perceives the therapist, fantasies about him and her expectations from the relationship with him. These are painful topics for the patient who may terminate treatment at this time. However, it is also a valuable opportunity to learn about her destructive pattern of involvement with inappropriate partners.

Consultation with a colleague is a wise move when confronted with a seductive patient, especially when the therapist is troubled by his feelings. With the rare patient who persists in seeking a sexual relationship, referral may be the only option.

The Vulnerable Therapist

Men are attracted to women and vice-versa. Therapists are fallible human beings. They are more likely to be attracted to a patient when they are unhappily married and their own sex lives are unsatisfactory. Sometimes the therapist has a patient come into the office who is "the woman of his dreams." He had been searching for her all his life but never expected to find her.

Therapists are also vulnerable in the following situation:

A woman patient who is very attractive to him is in a marriage, or other relationship, and is being abused. The therapist finds that he is preoccupied with rescue fantasies. Instead of listening with an open mind, such thoughts intrude as: "This 'poor dear' doesn't deserve to be treated so shabbily. If she were my wife, I would certainly appreciate what I have and treat her differently."

Prevention

The best method of insuring that the ethical boundaries between therapist and patient are not violated is early detection and prevention. When feelings of love, desire and passion become intense, good judgment and intelligent decisions may be impossible. Rationalizations and unrealistic expectations take over. Experience and intelligence are no guarantees that this cannot happen. Not a few outstanding psychiatrists have been guilty of ethical lapses.

The guideline that, except for a handshake, therapists and patients should not touch is a good one but not always easy to follow. There are times when the patient, after much effort and struggle, has succeeded in a very important endeavor and in a burst of enthusiasm, hugs the therapist. It would be churlish for the therapist to push the patient away. Or, if a patient, who is moving out of town after a lengthy period of therapy where much has been accomplished, asks "May I kiss you goodbye?" What should the therapist do? If the therapist is clear in his own mind where the boundaries are, he will not go wrong when he acts like a human being. Even Freud on occasion would say: "That was such a good insight that I will celebrate by lighting up a cigar."

Therapists need to be alert to distinguish between a good relationship that moves therapy along and when it begins to become too intense. If the patient begins to dress provocatively, this needs to be discussed ("Your taste in clothes seems to be changing.") Dreams also give early indications of growing involvement and an opportunity to analyze.

Probably most important of all, is for the therapist to recognize when personal problems interfere with his ability to listen to patients without jeopardizing the ethical boundaries. He may be pleasantly surprised to find that psychotherapy helps. Therapy for the therapist is a good investment.

Clinical Illustration

The patient was a woman in her mid-thirties, moderately depressed and going through a stormy period in the relationship with her boyfriend. She was articulate and had a lot to say. On the second visit, she spoke at length about how sad she felt that she recently had to "put down" her old dog. She asked the therapist whether he liked dogs, and he said that he had two of them. At the end of the session, the patient said: "You're so easy to talk to. Maybe we can go out for a drink sometime?" The therapist was very uncomfortable and didn't know what to say. The therapist was a first year resident, and this had not happened to him before.

The therapist discussed this with his supervisor who made some suggestions. On the patient's next visit, at an appropriate time, he asked: "Tell me about the boy-friend. I don't have a clear picture of him." The patient described him as withdrawn, distant and rather cold. The therapist asked what she thought of him. She said he came across as sympathetic, kind, warm and mature. The therapist then suggested that these were qualities she valued and hoped to find in the men she cared about. He added that, as she probably knew, it would not be ethical to have a relationship with a patient aside from the therapeutic one. The therapist was not too uncomfortable nor was the patient.

Chapter 14

HOW TO BECOME A BETTER THERAPIST

As with any professional discipline, the psychotherapist will be a student for the rest of his or her life. In spite of the many years of education involved in professional training, most will begin practice with insufficient experience in the technique of psychotherapy. The majority will join their professional organizations, read journals and books, go to meetings, lectures, attend seminars and workshops, and so on.

A few will enroll in psychoanalytic institutes where training is extensive, intensive and expensive. Most institutes require a lengthy personal analysis and three supervised analyses. In addition, there are courses, lectures and seminars. Only a few will feel that this is a good investment in the light of current economic conditions.

There are other options. In larger cities, there are shorter courses and workshops given by various organizations and graduate departments of universities. There are excellent summer courses given by the Menninger Clinic, the Albert Einstein College of Medicine in New York, the Cape Cod Symposia run by the New England Educational Institute in Pittsfield, Massachusetts, and many others.

There is no substitute for experience. We learn most by doing, i.e. working with patients. Learning psychotherapy has many characteristics of an apprenticeship. We need one to one supervision. However it is arranged, I recommend that the beginning therapist arrange for supervision and consultation with a more experienced colleague for at least the first one or two years in practice. In other specialties we send the patient to the consultant, but in psychotherapy it works out better for the therapist to go and avoid complicating the patient-therapist relationship.

THE AGING OF A THERAPIST

There are some who are good therapists from the very beginning, but all get better with more experience. In my opinion, therapists get better with age. The peak years for a surgeon may be 30-60, but therapists keep on getting better until senility or Alzheimer's catches up with them. The practice of psychotherapy is a growth experience, it is an occupational benefit. Therapists learn along with their patients.

As they age, therapists become less doctrinaire, more independent of their theories and less easily frustrated by patients. They develop better judgment and help patients set more realistic goals: that you have to wait for some things, you can't have it now and you can't have it all—above all, to help patients accept themselves. They don't have to live up to the expectations of others, or of themselves. We don't dislike ourselves because we are inferior. It's the other way around, we feel inferior because we dislike ourselves.

A PLACE FOR LITERATURE AND THE ARTS

The psychotherapist is not only a specialist, he is also a generalist. He is a member of the larger community and needs to be aware of what's happening in the world. Contemporary novelists and playwrights express the feelings, hopes and conflicts of people far better than clinicians. All art forms, especially the movies, are significant expressions of the society we live in.

In high school and college we were exposed to the great classics of literature but couldn't fully appreciate them. We no longer need them to pass courses and obtain degrees, but they are invaluable in providing insight into human character and motivation. They are also exciting reading. I strongly urge psychotherapists to renew their acquaintance with them.

I would especially recommend the plays of Shakespeare, Ibsen, Chekhov, George Bernard Shaw, Eugene O'Neill, Tennessee Williams and Arthur Miller. Also the novels of Dickens, Hawthorne, Dostoyevsky, Somerset Maugham and Albert Camus. A special favorite of mine is Lewis Carroll. "Alice's Adventures in Wonderland" and "Through the Looking Glass" express profound truths with whimsy and gentle humor. This is a very incomplete list, and I have not mentioned any of the fine contemporary writers.

I would like to call attention to a group of writers who teach English, History, Linguistics, and other subjects at various universities and are also serious students of psychoanalysis. Their discussion of some of the major works of literature provides an additional dimension because of their competence in both fields. I will mention only two works in the considerable literature: "Poems In Persons" by N.N. Holland (Columbia University Press, Morningside Edition, 1989) and "Imagined Human Beings" by B.J. Paris (New York University Press, 1997).

The extensive religious literature should not be overlooked. Many of these works contain profound insights and wisdom. Aside from its religious aspects, the Bible belongs among the masterpieces of world literature. Many psychologists and psychiatrists have borrowed extensively from teachings of the Eastern religions. One of my favorite quotations is from the Talmud:

If I am not for myself, who will be for me?
If I am only for myself, what am I?
If not now—when?

GLOSSARY

These are terms and concepts which may be of interest to psychotherapists. It is not a complete list, only the more common terms in the literature are included.

Abreaction: The emotional release which occurs after recalling a previously repressed, or suppressed, painful experience. Intellectual recall is not enough, it must be accompanied by the appropriate emotion. In the early days of psychoanalysis, abreaction was considered the primary therapeutic mode. In contemporary practice, it is considered of much lesser importance than insight and transference. Also called *catharsis.*

Acting-out: Expressing unconscious material by behavior rather than by speech. The person is not aware of the full significance of his actions which are frequently harmful to others and damaging to himself. Acting-out blocks insight and is antitherapeutic.

Affect: The subjective experience of emotion accompanying thoughts and ideas. It is described as appropriate or inappropriate depending on its relation to the thought content. The terms blunted or flat are applied when there is lessened or absent emotional expression. It is also used as a general term for feeling and emotion.

Alienation: The intrapsychic process which results in the distancing of a person from his own feelings, wishes and beliefs. The individual is estranged from his real self, he is a "stranger to himself."

Ambivalent: The simultaneous presence of conflicting feelings and attitudes, e.g. feeling love and hate for the same person.

Anal Character: A person who is excessively orderly, miserly and stubborn. According to Freudian theory, these personality traits have their origin in the anal phase of development which occurs in the first and second years of life.

Analysis: Another term for *psychoanalysis.*

Analytic Psychology: The name given to his psychological theory and therapy by Carl Jung (1875-1961). Originally a collaborator of Freud's, he broke away to start his own school. He made great contributions to the study of myths, symbolism, interpretation of dreams, and the study of character. He coined the terms introvert and extrovert, and the collective unconscious.

Analyze: The process of examining thought, feeling and behavior in order to understand their significance. See also *insight* and *interpretation.*

Anxiety: A distressing emotion of uneasiness and apprehension, similar to fear but without a recognized danger. Anxiety has a crucial role in producing conflict and neurotic symptoms. In Freudian theory, unconscious fantasies of punishment for instinctual wishes originated in childhood. There are four cardinal dangers: (1) loss of love, (2) loss of the love-object, (3) castration (impotence) and (4) superego condemnation (failure to live up to expectations).

"As If" Personality: The person lacks the capacity for appropriate emotional expression, but appears to the casual observer "as if" he does. This results from a severe character disorder.

Body Image: The sense of one's own body; the mental representation of one's body. It is distorted in many mental disorders, e.g. the starving anorectic patient who experiences herself as fat, the beautiful woman who feels she is ugly.

Character: The relatively stable personality traits and modes of reacting. Sometimes used interchangeably with *personality.*

Character Disorders: A group of pathological emotional disturbances which are manifested by disordered behavior patterns rather than by specific symptoms. In DSM-IV, they are classified in Axis II as personality disorders. In the literature the term is often used to refer to psychopathic (antisocial) personality.

Castration: Fear of loss or injury to the genitals; fantasied loss of the genitals. Also used to denote impotence, loss of power, helplessness or humiliation.

Cathexis: The investment of psychic energy (libido) in an idea or image. The process is conscious and unconscious.

Confrontation: The technique of inviting a patient to examine some aspect of her own behavior, e.g. repeating verbatim what the patient has just said.

Consciousness: The awareness of perceptions coming from the external world and from within one's own body.

Conversion: The unconscious defense mechanism in which intrapsychic conflicts are transformed into somatic symptoms, e.g. paralysis, pain, blindness, etc.

Countertransference: Similar to *transference* but going in the opposite direction, i.e. from therapist to patient. The therapist displaces onto the patient attitudes and feelings derived from earlier experiences in her (the therapist's) own life.

Defense: Usually refers to unconscious mechanisms which provide relief from anxiety. In analytic terms, the defenses which protect the ego from instinctual demands of the id. The defenses include: repression, displacement, reaction formation, isolation of affect, denial, somatization and conversion.

Denial: A primitive defense mechanism in which the person refuses to, or cannot, become aware of a painful reality, e.g. the wife who refuses to see the obvious signs of her husband's alcoholism.

Depersonalization: A disturbance in the sense of self; feelings of unfamiliarity with one's own body or body parts.

Derealization: Feeling detached from the environment. Often goes together with *depersonalization.*

Displacement: A defense mechanism in which feelings and attitudes are transferred from their original source to another person. It occurs in transference, phobias and dreams.

Dissociation: A splitting off of mental content from consciousness, as happens in conversion hysteria. Also, the splitting of emotional from cognitive aspects of an experience.

Drive: Basic urge or instinct. In Freudian theory, the instinctual drives were sexual and aggressive.

Dyad: A relationship involving two persons.

Ego: One of the three major structures of the mental apparatus in psychoanalytic theory. It maintains contact with the external world and mediates between the instinctual drives of the id and the personal and social prohibitions of the superego.

Ego Boundaries: The ability to differentiate real from unreal.

Ego-Dystonic: Attitudes and behavior that are not acceptable to the person. Also called *ego-alien.*

Ego Psychology: This was a successor to the earliest psychoanalytic orientation which focused on the instinctual drives of the id. Ego psychology emphasized the conscious aspects of the ego and its expanded functions. The ego was the agency responsible for adaptation and organizing mental processes into meaningful experience. Its major functions included: speech, memory, reality testing, mastery and judgment. There was recognition that development did not stop with resolution of the Oedipus complex. In therapy, more attention now was paid to current events and less on events of early childhood.

Ego Ideal: The image of the self to which the person strives to live up to. It has conscious and unconscious aspects. The term "idealized image," coined by Karen Horney (*Neurosis and Human Growth*, New York, W.W. Norton, 1950) is frequently encountered in the literature and is essentially the same concept.

Ego-Syntonic: Attitudes and behavior that are acceptable to the person.

Empathy: Awareness of the feelings and behavior of another person. It is an "emotional knowing" of another person; it is not intellectual and is different from sympathy.

Existential Psychotherapy: Another school of therapy that evolved from psychoanalysis and is related to existential philosophy. It is defined by I.D. Yalom as: "A dynamic approach to therapy which focuses on concerns that are rooted in the individual's existence" (*Existential Psychotherapy*, New York, Basic Books, 1980).

Fantasy: Imagined events or images which gratify wishes; may be conscious (daydreams) or unconscious.

Fixation: Arrest of psychosexual development at a certain stage, e.g. oral, anal, or phallic.

Free Association: The spontaneous verbalization of everything that comes to mind without selection or censorship. This is a basic procedure in analysis and other expressive therapies.

Genital Phase: The final phase of psychosexual development which begins at puberty and indicates emotional maturity and the capacity for intimacy and object love.

Hysteria: A neurosis characterized by conversion and dissociative symptoms. The symptoms are disguised substitutes for the gratification of unconscious drives. Also called conversion hysteria.

Id: One of the three main mental structures in classical analytic theory; the domain of unconscious instinctual drives.

Identification: The unconscious mental process whereby a person becomes like another person in some aspect. This is different from imitation and role modeling which are conscious functions.

Identity: A person's sense of self; the experience of the self as a unique entity which persists over time.

Identity Crisis: Conflict over adapting to the role expected by society at times of rapid social change or when there is a marked increase in strength of instinctual drives.

Imprinting: Behavioral patterning which occurs at critical points in early development. The term was derived from ethology and originally applied to animal behavior.

Impulse Disorder: A large group of disorders characterized by difficulties with control of instinctual drives, e.g. kleptomania, addictions and sexual perversions.

Individual Psychology: The name given to the psychological system of theory and therapy originated by Alfred Adler (1870-1937). At one time a collaborator of Freud, he developed his own theory which emphasized compensation for feelings of inferiority (inferiority complex) and the drive for power.

Individuation: The process of development which occurs over the period from 6 months to 3 years of age and results in the differentiation of the mental representations of self from that of the mother. The goal is the development of the individual personality. Also called the process of *sep-aration-individuation.*

Insight: Self-knowledge, understanding the significance and meaning of one's thinking and behavior.

Interpretation: The intervention by the therapist which results in the patient's understanding some aspect of his problems or behavior; the process of achieving insight.

Introjection: The unconscious defense mechanism whereby external objects, or object-representations, are absorbed within oneself. The converse of projection. The terms identification, incorporation and introjection are similar and not clearly differentiated from each other.

Latency: In analytic literature, the period from 5-6 years to puberty during which the sexual drive is relatively inactive.

Libido: The energy of the sexual drive in classic analytic theory. Libido theory held that there was a sequence of developmental phases: oral, anal, phallic and genital. Libido can be invested (cathected) in the intrapsychic representation of objects (object libido), or of the self (narcissism).

Metapsychology: Academic psychology of the late 19th and early 20th centuries equated "mental" with "conscious." Freud used the term metapsychology to indicate that psychoanalytic theories went beyond conscious experience.

Narcissism: The term indicates a concentration of psychologic interest upon the self. It comes from the legend of Narcissus and means self-love. It is a broad term, and sometimes "healthy narcissism" is used to indicate pride and self-esteem. Usually the term is used to indicate some degree of emotional disturbance due to excessive concern for the self.

Neurosis: Synonymous with psychoneurosis. A large group of mental disorders, distinct from psychosis, characterized by maladaptive patterns of behavior, persistent disturbance of mood, physical symptoms without discoverable cause, and so on. They correspond loosely to DSM-IV categories of dysthymia, anxiety disorders, somatoform disorders, dissociative disorders, adjustment disorders and personality disorders. In almost all patients, the disturbance involves Axis I and II.

Object: The analytic term for a person other than the self. The person whom an individual loves is the love-object. It is an awkward term but continues to be widely used and is frequently encountered in the literature.

Object Relations Theory: In the past few decades, analysts have developed an alternative theoretical system which they feel is more helpful with some patients. Based to some extent on contributions of Harry Stack Sullivan (1892-1949), it was essentially developed by Melanie Klein (1882-1960) and other members of the British Psychoanalytic Society.

In classical theory the drives are primary, but in Object Relations theory, relationships are primary. Drives develop only in the context of a relationship and may be directed toward objects for specific reasons rather than for tension reduction (gratification). In the course of development, entire interpersonal relationships are internalized, i.e. self-representations and object-representations. Conflict may develop between opposing sets of relationships.

Splitting of the ego is an important defense mechanism to protect what can't be tolerated at the time. Alternating cycles of projection and introjection occur until the images of self and objects are integrated, e.g. the "good mother" and the "bad mother" become one. At approximately 3 years of age, the representation of the unified "whole mother" can be internalized and sustains the child during the mother's absence. This is the beginning of object constancy. A parallel process goes on with the integration of the "good self" and "bad self" representations. If these processes are not completed successfully, there are character deficits which are carried over into adult life.

Object Relations theory has proven to be more helpful in understanding borderline and narcissistic personality disorders. The quality of therapy with these patients improves with greater emphasis on relationships. The role of the therapist also changes. In addition to functioning as a "blank screen" and as an object of transference, she is also a new object to be internalized and bolster deficits in the character structure.

Oedipus Complex: The crucial complex in Freudian theory, named after the Greek myth. In its simplest form, a male child at the height of the phallic phase (3-6 years) has sexual strivings for the mother and fears retaliation (castration) by the father. Successful resolution of the conflict occurs with sublimation of the child's drives and aims, and identification with the father's ethics and values. "The heir of the oedipal conflict is the superego (conscience)." Failure to successfully negotiate this phase of development leads to neurosis and continuing conflict.

Oral Stage: The stage of psychosexual stage of development from birth to 18 months of age when the needs and modes of expression are centered in the mouth. Generally divided into oral-dependent and oral-aggressive (biting) phases.

Over-determination: Clinical symptoms and behavior result from multiple causes reinforcing each other.

Penis Envy: The discontent of women with their own gender. It is now generally held that the discontent of women is realistically based on societal discrimination against women.

Personality: The totality of a person's thoughts, emotions and behavior in adapting to the environment. Often used as synonymous with *character*.

Phallic Phase: The period from 3 to 6 years during which the sexual interest centers about the genitals.

Phobia: A persistent, intense and unrealistic fear of an object or situation. It is believed to result from displacement of an unconscious conflict onto an external object which has an association with the conflict.

Pleasure Principle: The individual seeks pleasure and avoidance of pain. Conflict arises when gratification of needs would involve external or internal dangers. The young child operates by the pleasure principle but as he matures gives more consideration to the conditions of the external world and begins to act in accordance with the *reality principle.*

Preconscious: These are ideas, memories and images which are close to achieving consciousness. In the topographic model of the mind, it is the area between conscious and unconscious.

Pre-Oedipal Phase: The period from birth to approximately 3-4 years of age; before the onset of the Oedipus complex. When applied to the clinical picture, it implies that the disturbance originated early in development and is severe, e.g. narcissistic personality disorders, eating disorders, and addictions.

Primal Scene: The child's recollection, or fantasy, of adults engaged in sexual intercourse. The analytic literature emphasizes the potential traumatic impact of this on the child's subsequent development.

Primary Process: Primitive, unconscious thought processes associated with the instinctual drives; the realm of the *id.*

Projection: A defense mechanism in which unacceptable material is unconsciously rejected and attributed to others.

Projective Identification: An important defense mechanism in object relations theory. It is a 3-step process: (1) a self or object-representation is projected onto another object, (2) the object identifies with, and modifies, what is projected, and (3) the modified material is returned to the person by reintrojection.

Splitting and projective identification are interrelated, and both function to keep "good" and "bad" representations separated. The distinction between projection and projective identification is controversial; some authorities feel that the distinction between them is not significant.

Psychic Determinism: Psychological events follow strict laws, they do not result from chance; present events are determined by past events.

Psychoanalysis: This refers to three things: (1) a system of treatment of mental disorders, (2) a comprehensive psychologic theory of human development and behavior, and (3) a research method. Psychoanalysis, sometimes analysis for short, was founded by Sigmund Freud (1856-1939). He was influenced by the scientific climate of the time, especially Darwin's Theory of Evolution and the principle of conservation of energy.

The earliest theory, for a brief period, was the topographic: unconscious, conscious and preconscious. The classic theory is known as the drive/structure theory. The drives are sexual (libidinal) and aggressive, the structures: ego, id and superego. Treatment concentrated on events in childhood, free association and the recall of traumatic memories. Analysis of resistance and transference were defining features of the treatment. Interpretation of dreams was the "royal road to the unconscious."

Later developments emphasized the problems of adaptation and expanded the role of the ego. There was greater emphasis on current events and relationships. This perspective was called *Ego Psychology*. In the past several decades, we have seen the development of *Object Relations* theory and *Self Psychology*. These latter two developments now constitute the mainstream of the analytic movement. Therapists now have the flexibility to adapt theory to the individual patient and not forcibly fit the patient into a rigid theoretical position.

Mention should be made of the dissidents who left the "official" psychoanalytic movement but made great contributions to theory and therapy. The earliest were Alfred Adler and Carl Jung; much later came H.S. Sullivan, Eric Fromm and Karen Horney. The latter three are referred to as neo-Freudians or the culturalists. They were the forerunners of many later developments, but their contributions were not often acknowledged. What analysts did in actual practice was often quite different from what they described in their writings. Many were much better therapists than their theories would indicate.

Reality Principle: The ability to act in accordance with the conditions and demands of the external world; to postpone gratification to a more appropriate time.

Repetition Compulsion: The impulse to repeat earlier, often painful, emotional experiences irrespective of gain and pleasure.

Repression: The major unconscious defense mechanism in neurosis; thoughts, fantasies, and affects are pushed out of awareness and prevented from entering consciousness. Not to be confused with *suppression* which is a conscious process.

Resistance: The conscious and unconscious defenses against bringing up unacceptable or painful material into consciousness thereby blocking treatment. The defenses of the ego operate as resistance. In a general sense, it is the difficulties the patient has of being a patient.

Secondary Gain: The advantages of being ill, e.g. personal attention, relief of responsibility, compensation, etc.

Secondary Process: Thought processes which are orderly and logical, influenced by conditions in the environment and characteristic of the ego. Contrast with *primary process*.

Self: One of the most difficult terms to define; a few consider it as synonymous with the ego or "embedded" in the ego. Kohut's later definition of the self was: "the primary psychic constellation, the center of experience and initiative and the main motivating agency."

Self Object: Discussed with *Self Psychology*.

Self Psychology: The later psychoanalytic theory that was derived from the treatment of narcissistic personality disorders by Heinz Kohut (1913-1981) and his followers. There are many similarities with Object Relation theory which it complements. Self Psychology emphasizes the external relationships necessary to maintain the integrity of the self, while object relations emphasized the internalized relations of self- and object-representations.

The patients exhibited three characteristic transference reactions: mirroring, idealizing and twinship. In mirroring, the person is trying to obtain a confirming or validating response from the therapist (and originally from the mother). In the idealizing transference, the patient perceives the therapist as the ideal, powerful parent and basks in the reflected glory. The twinship, or kinship, transference reaction represents the need of the patient to be like the therapist in some aspects. The etiology of the deficits in the integrity of the self was the failure of empathy in the mother who did not adequately respond to the needs of the child.

In describing relationships, an important concept is that of the *selfobject*. The selfobject is not a separate person but the function that other persons have in fulfilling the needs of an individual. Relationships with others is a *self-selfobject* relationship. The individual never outgrows his need for self objects, but with maturity he gives up the archaic ones and relates to more appropriate ones.

Splitting: An unconscious, primitive defense mechanism that separates contradictory self-representations and object-representations, e.g. splits the "good self" from the "bad self." It is a primitive defense mechanism and characteristic of borderline personality disorders.

The term *splitting of the ego* is also encountered in the literature and refers to splitting of the functions of the ego into the experiencing function and the observing function.

Structural Theory: The classic Freudian theory that the psychic apparatus consists of 3 structures: ego, id and superego.

Superego: The superego is manifested by conscience, morals and sense of guilt. It results from identification with the attitudes of parents.

Thought Disorder: A disturbance in the content of thought and communication, e.g. delusions, loosening of associations, ideas of reference, etc.

Transference: The displacement of patterns of feelings and behavior originally experienced with significant persons of childhood onto current relationships. It results in misinterpretation of the present in terms of the past. Usually used to describe the feelings of the patient for the therapist. Countertransference is the same process going in the opposite direction, from therapist to patient.

Transference Neurosis: An old term for those neuroses which were amenable to treatment by analysis. They included hysteria, phobias, obsessions and compulsions. This was to distinguish the group from the *narcissistic neuroses* which could not be treated. This latter term would now be called the psychoses.

Transitional Object: The child's first toy, or blanket, at the time he or she begins to be aware that the mother is a separate person. The child clings to this as a link with the mother.

Working Through: The term used by Freud to describe the process of repetition of some phase of analytic work in order to bring about lasting change in the patient.

Unconscious: A descriptive term to indicate mental functioning which is out of awareness. It is the repository of data which was conscious and then repressed, as well as data which has never been conscious.

INDEX

103